quick art

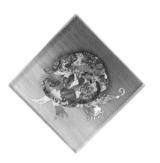

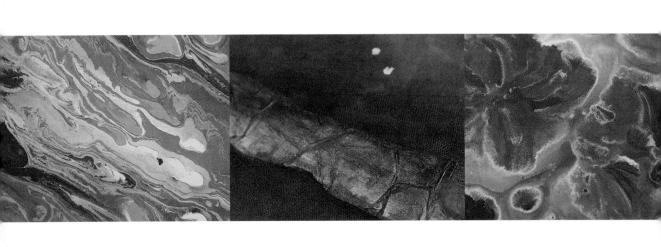

art of the ordinary

quick art

angie franke and monique day-wilde

METZ PRESS

Most of the photographs taken on location at Latreuo Guest House in Welgemoed (www. comfortstay.co.za) and Bobby Breen Interiors (www.bobbybreen.co.za)

Published by Metz Press
1 Cameronians Avenue
Welgemoed, 7530 South Africa

First published in 2006
Second printing 2007
Third printing 2008
Copyright © Metz Press 2006, 2007, 2008
Text and templates copyright © Angie Franke and Monique Day-Wilde
Photographs copyright © Metz Press

Publisher	Wilsia Metz
Design and lay-out	Lindie Metz
Photographer	Ivan Naudé
Reproduction	Color/Fuzion
Print production	Les Martens, SA Media Services, Cape Town

Printed and bound in Singapore by Star Standard
ISBN 10: 1-919992-46-4
ISBN 13: 978-1-919992-46-4

Contents

Acknowledgements

Thank YOU for buying our book! We hope this inspires you to explore your own creative journey. We know that experiencing art, even more than its outcome, brings joy and satisfaction.

WE ARE SO GRATEFUL TO OUR MUSES AND SUPPORTERS

Grenvor Wilde and Tessa Cudmore for being such loving moms and thinking we're wonderful, no matter what we produce: we love (and can see through) your polite smiles at some of our endeavours!

Ted Cudmore: Thanks, Pop, for being my first and constant source of inspiration, help, lateral thinking, and enthusiasm for crafts.

Michael Day, your support and thoughtfulness continue to amaze me!

Michael Tristan and Joshua, whose honest critique and practical support I couldn't do without – thanks for all the tea!

Michael Franke – for all you do, and for your support of our family.

John, Elizabeth Louise and Gemma Rose for your loving help and forgiveness – and honest art criticism!

Peter Weisswange – for everything – my muse and support.

Xoliswa Maureen Yozo and Nondumiso Gloria Qobo for your bright smiles and untiring dedication – even when you weren't sure what you were washing up!

Our extended family and friends who helped with so many things, especially Sue Burton, Lynn and Malcolm Connolly, Debbie and Richard Cook, Cherylee Jordaan, Clara and Anthony Klitsie, Sarie Marais, Bernie Millar, Moira-Lee Purdon, Liz van Aarde, Lindsay Woods.

We also thank: Suan and Dale Landman, Shelagh Johnston, Hans Rijs of Siseko Distributors, for all the carting around!

Carmel and Bernhard Wolf of Sherwood Garden Centre, Dot Bowker of Bowker Arts and Crafts, Frank Lyall for Art supports, Pam Black of Africote and all the Ivans – they know who they are!

Mr. G.B. Rudd and the 6E class of Mount Pleasant Primary.

And to all those who broke their heads over our paint and maths formulae.

Thanks to Pam and Bobby Breen of Bobby Breen Interiors, Jaco Brand of Latreuo guest house, Wilsia and Ralf Metz, Lindie Metz and Gwen Nel for allowing us to invade your spaces.

We are grateful to Lindie for enhancing our work with such a creative and exciting book design.

And most especially thanks to Wilsia Metz for indulging and promoting us in yet another creative endeavour.

I wish to thank my parents for making it all possible...and I wish to thank my children for making it necessary.

Victor Borge

Introduction

Departing from tradition, our own and the broader arts and crafts scene, we have responded to the overwhelming interest in home décor in the broadest sense, from soft furnishings to wall art.

After the publication of our book on fabric painting, we felt the need for a change. We both really like the idea of using things in a different way than for what they were originally intended, experimenting with whatever we can find. While living in different cities, we often have simultaneous 'Aha!' moments and started working on new ideas – together, but apart. Angie did her thing using painted Supawood panels Velcro-ed to a wall, allowing the panels to be re-positioned as often as the mood dictates, while Monique experimented with crack filler and three-dimensional shapes – and a new book was born!

The accent is on texture, line and colour to create easy and effective ideas, with the additions of pastes, crack filler, cements, oxides, sand, metal filings, rust paint and everything but the kitchen sink – though there are some washers in here somewhere! Using left-over wall paint you can change your interior by applying simple techniques like dribbling, dripping and even throwing meths onto it and waiting for a reaction. For canvases we've used whatever supports happened to be handy – an old door, a rusty gate, wooden panels, an old magnetic board ... you name it, we used it. The more traditional acrylics and oils haven't been forgotten either, with our own spin on paint by numbers and plastic supports.

We've found wonderful inspiration for our work by looking at the world around us a little differently: from the repeating rhythm of a long stretch of wire fencing to the smallest details of shells and flowers. We've looked at other art works with interested, analytical and critical eyes, in terms of colour combinations, pattern, texture, shape and effects. We must stress that using other people's work as inspiration and a springboard for your own ideas is fine – copying directly is not, unless permission is given. Most printed matter will have a copyright logo ©, which means it is illegal to copy. Books, like this one, will usually have a note saying that it is fine to copy designs for personal use, but not reproduce them for any commercial gain (this includes teaching).

Sometimes we've found details of artwork more interesting than the whole. These have led to wonderful ideas which we've developed further. Paying attention to detail on finished work can make all the difference. Adding just a little more dark shading, texture or embellishments to finish an article can take it from the mundane to a real work of art. However, it is important to know when to stop!

This book aims to bridge the gap between craft and art, using craft techniques to create and indulge in original art – things that anyone can do.

James A.M. Whistler said: "Art happens. No hovel is safe from it, no prince can depend on it, the vastest intelligence cannot bring it about." If you want to, you will!

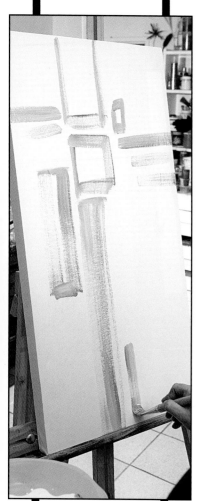

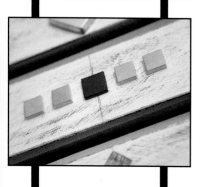

Materials

When you create art, you can use anything that happens to be handy to paint on or decorate, from wood and glass to the traditional canvas. Different mediums can be used as paint or added to paint to create interesting textures. Traditionally paint is applied with a brush. Again, use whatever you have at hand, from a paintbrush to your fingers.

Supports

WOOD

All wood-based products need careful priming and sealing primers depending on where they would be used, for example in outdoor areas.

MDF/SUPAWOOD

Medium-density fibre-board is our preferred support. It comes in varying thicknesses from 3 mm up. One generally has to buy a large board, so plan your projects accordingly. Most suppliers will cut board for a fee.

MASONITE

Also known as hardboard, masonite, too, is available in varying thicknesses from 3 mm up. It is smooth on one side and may be pre-painted; the rough side has a canvas-like pattern imprinted into it, which, when primed, makes a cheap substitute for painting canvases.

CHIPBOARD

This is sometimes called pressboard as it is less dense than MDF and hardboard. Once cut it should be primed as soon a possible to prevent it from swelling and crumbling.

PLYWOOD

Plywood consists of thin layers of wood veneer which have been placed with the grain of each layer running crosswise with the next for strength. The layers are heated and pressure-bonded with strong glue. These wood 'sandwiches' are supplied in varying thicknesses (graded for indoor or outdoor use) and are stronger and heavier than wood of the same size.

CANVAS

Available by the metre in different weights and widths, it can be glued or stretched onto frames or supports. Bear in mind that it will stretch with time, and also the weight of art materials applied to it.

If you do stretch your own canvas it will need to be primed with two coats of a good quality primer. It is much easier to buy them ready-made from an art shop. Canvases are available in a myriad of sizes.

OTHER

Paper, cardboard, soft board (pin board) stone, vinyl, perspex, melamine, cement, brick, metal, tiles, mirrors and styrofoam sheets are all interesting supports. You may have junk lying around which can be used to practise on, rather than buying expensive supports. Indulge in some creative scavenging – like we did!

Texture mediums

All mediums discussed here can be applied to a chosen support using some of the painting tools mentioned in that section. For most projects we have used scrapers or brushes to apply the medium. These mediums can all be mixed with water, glue, paint, oxides and pigments. While they dry with different textures, they all hold their shape as applied.

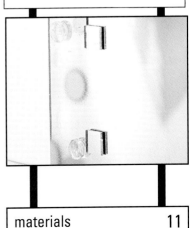

CRETE STONE

This is fine, gritty, cement-like powder which can be mixed with water, glue, paint, oxides and pigments and applied to strong, rigid supports. It dries to a rough texture and does not shrink. Before decorating, check the entire surface carefully to see that the plaster has set.

CRACK FILLER

Crack filler is a smooth paste, bought ready-mixed or in powder form that is mixed with water. It dries to a smooth finish and does not shrink.

TEXTURE PASTE

This may also be sold as modelling paste, is usually white in colour and dries white. It may be applied to any surface to give an impasto finish. It is available in smooth, textured or fancy finishes. While it holds it applied shape, it does shrink on drying. Texture paste is also used to sculpt and is strong enough to hold objects impressed into it.

GEL MEDIUM

Gel medium appears white or clear, but always dries clear and is available in matt or gloss finish. It shrinks a good deal while drying and has similar properties to texture paste, but is not as robust. It has the advantage of retaining the clarity of any colour added to it.

SAND (BUILDERS OR BEACH)

Sand is a simple additional texture, which has the distinct advantage of being freely available (and free – ours was unwittingly donated by the builders across the road). We suggest adding a collection of different grades and colour of sand to different binders, as we did in our projects. It can also be mixed into paint, painted over or sprinkled onto wet paint for very different textures.

Paint

Paint consists of a colour (pigment), mixed with a glue (base), to stick it onto a surface. The type of base used to bond the colour is determined by the surface to be coated and the durability required. Generally paints are either water-based or oil-based.

Oil-based paints may be painted over the water-based variety but not vice versa. While we give general descriptions of and application instructions for various paints, it is always important to follow the specific manufacturer's instructions for their particular products.

Undercoats and primers

All surfaces need to be prepared for painting, including those for art! Undercoats and primers act as a barrier coat, as well as a bond between the support surface and the paint, forming a "ground" for paint application.

There are many undercoats available, but we favour the water-based products. There is a water-based undercoat/primer which doubles as a filler/crack sealer and undercoat. This has a chalky, matt finish, which adheres to most surfaces and can be overcoated with emulsion or oil. Universal undercoat, however, has a slight sheen to it when dry. The solvent for universal undercoat is mineral turpentine. Before using any of these products, read the instructions on the label, as they vary.

Gesso

Gesso is generally found in acrylic form in art shops but traditionally it was made from a combination of rabbit-hide glue and titanium white mixed with water. In paste form it is used to build relief, while thinned it becomes a multipurpose primer suited for canvases, furniture and objects. Alternatively, use spackle, a very smooth, economical crack filler found at most hardware stores. For extra adhesion, add a little wood glue.

PVA/Acrylic

Polyvinyl acetate/acrylic is basically wood glue with pigment and chalk added. It is water-based and dries to a flexible plastic finish, if it is a good quality. Generally it needs two coats for good cover and dries quickly to a matt finish. Many new variations dry to a soft sheen. These paints are economical and are available in a wide range of colours and quantities. While these may be diluted with water when liquid, they are permanent and water resistant when dry.

The greatest masterpieces were once only pigments on a palette.
Henry S. Haskins

Oil/enamel

Traditionally these paints are made from boiled linseed oil and pigment. They are extremely flexible and long lasting. Oils take a long time to dry. They dry to a smooth, shiny finish, and usually only require one coat to cover. Eggshell enamels have a matt finish. Use mineral turpentine to thin these paints or clean equipment (see solvents, page 18). Oil enamel paints are not cheap, have a limited colour range and are not easily available in small quantities. The new range of water-based enamels, however, make using this product much more versatile, and will surely replace the old fashioned kind in popularity.

Special effects paints

CEMENT PAINT

With the Tuscan look here to stay, this range of liquid cement-based-paint is worth investigating. The paint is available in earth tones and dries very quickly to a chalky cement finish. We experimented by adding bright pigments and this works well too. These paints can be scratched into as for plaster Scraffito. They are very affordable and come in powder or liquid form but, once mixed, have a short shelf life. As they have been developed for exterior wall finishes, they need to be sealed with matt or gloss water-based glaze-coat for interior work, otherwise they gather much dust.

CHALKBOARD PAINT

This is available in various colours, but traditionally in black and green. It creates a smooth, non-reflective surface which can be written on with chalk. It may be used on wood, metal or walls, which have been suitably primed. The particles suspended in this paint settle quickly, so it is advisable to stir consistently during the painting process. A new magnetic variation is available, enabling you to affix notes with magnets to the painted surface (so they claim!).

RUST PAINT

This paint is designed to look corroded and rusted. It is not cheap! There are various makes and all have different components and instructions. Basically rust paint requires iron filings in a paint base over a suitable stained undercoat. A liquid activator is brushed over the iron paint and left until the rust develops. Varnishing or sealing with a glaze coat when the desired effect has been achieved, will halt the rusting process and protect the paint surface from flaking.

Some rust paints are smooth and others textured, depending on the size of the iron filings or powder suspended in the paint. Activating fluids can produce a rust palette varying from yellow through orange, red and brown to black rust.

We've even experimented with making our own rust with iron filings in clear water-based varnish with salty water sloshed over and left to develop. (Grab some steelwool and your salt cellar and play with your cheese grater – we can't guarantee the results, but you'll have fun!)

COPPER PAINT

This is similar to rust paint. It also requires an activating fluid to bring out the lovely aged patina and verdigris (green/blue) colour to the copper particles suspended in the paint base. It too is costly and unfortunately not easily available in small quantities. We don't recommend making this in your kitchen, er … What would you shave up for copper filings?

METALLICS

These paints consist of metal powders added to water-based varnish – oil varnish results in a dull finish. If you need large quantities, you will find it more economical to make your own. Powders are available from most craft shops. Experiment with quantities.

PEARL

These are similar to metallic, but use powdered mica (pearl powders), to produce a lovely, soft lustre. Pigments may be added, but as the mica is white-based, they will result in pastel tones. Again our golden rule applies – experiment!

SPARKLE/GLITTER PAINT

Add coloured glitter or sparkle dust to water-based varnish to create wonderfully cheeky effects. Use what you have mixed as soon as possible – the colour can run from the glitter, if stored. Ready-made glitter paints are available in small quantities. Think out of the box and use up your teenager's discarded glitter nail-varnish. (We know a guilty mom or two!)

NEON

These bright, synthetic paints must be bought as is – they cannot be mixed from the primary colours. They are very appealing and funky for pop art and children's projects. Also very pricey, they are available in bottles and spray cans.

GLOW IN THE DARK (FLUORESCENT)

This is a water-based paint which glows gently after being "charged" by bright light or with black lighting. It requires at least three coats for maximum effect, and is most effective when stencilled, as it is very expensive. It may be applied to any primed surface – white undercoat is recommended.

FABRIC PAINT

All fabric paint, including puff and sun paints, are basically acrylic and can be used on most of the above supports as long as they are sealed correctly. They do have a tendency to fade.

SPRAY PAINT

Spray paint is available in many finishes, including enamel, antique, metallic and a wide range of colours, including neon and fluorescent

This beloved tool of all graffiti artists contains paint under extreme pressure. It has the advantage of easy application. No mess, no fuss!

GLAZES

Glaze is basically paint thinned with its relevant solvent, with the addition of a neutral medium to delay drying time. This enables the glaze to be worked into textural effects. Glaze appears milky or creamy when wet, but dries clear. It is transparent, adding depth to the base coat, and drying to a soft sheen. Scumble glaze is commercially available in oil and acrylic bases for use with enamel and PVA respectively, although you can make your own using artists' colours.

Solvents

A solvent or solvent medium is a basic constituent of the paint base, for example water is the main constituent for acrylic paint. Paints, varnishes, oils, grease and so on are dissolved by their relevant solvents. They are also used for thinning paint to glazes or washes, and are essential for cleaning equipment.

All solvents, except water, have a toxic effect in one way or another, and should be used with care, in well ventilated areas. Solvents are environmentally damaging and need to be dried out before being disposed of.

Hint: Use paper towel for cleaning and bag only when dry.

WATER
Check labels carefully before washing brushes, or diluting paint with water. Generally all acrylics are water-based and, as mentioned before, there are new oil paints which use water as a solvent.

MINERAL TURPENTINE
Also known as white spirits, this solvent is chemically based on the natural turpentine from the resin of pine trees. It is is used for diluting and cleaning enamel paint.

Hint: When diluting artists' oil paints, rather use natural (artists') turpentine, as mineral turps dulls the shiny oil paint finish.

LACQUER THINNERS
Lacquer thinners is extremely strong and rapidly deteriorates many surfaces and fabrics. It is used to dilute and clean up various lacquer products. Generally too caustic for all paints, lacquer thinners is often used for removing adhesive residue from a variety of surfaces.

Always test in an inconspicuous area before use.

METHYLATED SPIRITS
Methylated spirits is a type of denatured alcohol. Also known as methyl alcohol, this serves as a solvent for shellac flakes, as well as for some quick drying spirit based paints, for example glass paint. Shagreen and other solvent-release paint-techniques work well with this solvent.

ACETONE
Acetone is fast evaporating and is the same medium as nailpolish remover. It can be used as a thinner and cleaner and may be used as a solvent for epoxies, polyester, fibreglass resins, vinyl, lacquers and adhesives and will dissolve grease, oil, and wax.

PAINT STRIPPER AND COMMERCIAL DEGREASER

While the names of these products speak for themselves, they are a useful addition to your tool cupboard as they can rescue paint brushes which have stiffened with paint residue. These cleaners should be used with great care, as they are highly corrosive. Wipe dissolved paint residue onto kitchen paper for disposal, before rinsing the brushes in warm soapy water.

Hint: Another useful general solvent is ordinary white vinegar. Use it for brush cleaning and try mixing acrylic paint with it for vinegar painting.

Special additions

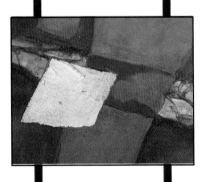

METALLIC LEAF

Traditionally used for gilding, these whisper thin sheets of metallic foil are used with a glue binder (gilding milk or size), to add lustrous highlights to any surface. The sheets are sold in booklets with tissue interleaving and come in a range of finishes, from expensive 9kt gold to Dutch metal and aluminium, copper and variegated colour. Leaf fragments known as skewings may also be bought for small projects. Protect your finished work with shellac varnish.

METALLIC POWDERS

Metal dust particles or glitter can be suspended in or blown onto paint or varnish to create wonderful shiny effects. These can be bought ready-mixed, or you can make your own by buying powders from a stamping supplier. Embossing powder, popular with card-makers and stampers, adheres to wet paint or size and are cured by direct heat, for example from a heat gun or element. While embossing powders look dull, once cured they have the effect of encrusting the surface with a raised metal layer.

SHELLAC

This is the original resin varnish, produced from the secretion of the Indian lac insect, and is sold in flakes or liquid form. It is usually clear or amber in colour and flakes are dissolved in denatured alcohol (methylated spirits). It is the recommended varnish for gilding as it prevents tarnishing. Shellac must be applied quickly, as it dries very fast. It is highly toxic, with a strong odour. Work in a well-ventilated area. The high sheen of original French polish is from shellac.

Other art materials

We love to experiment with all sorts of things scratched out of our cupboards and snuffled from shop shelves (say that fast ten times!). Don't forget about all the conventional things such as Kokis, liners, pastels and crayons and other odd useful stuff like dishwashing liquid (useful resist medium) or salt for a hygroscopic texturizer (dishwasher and table).

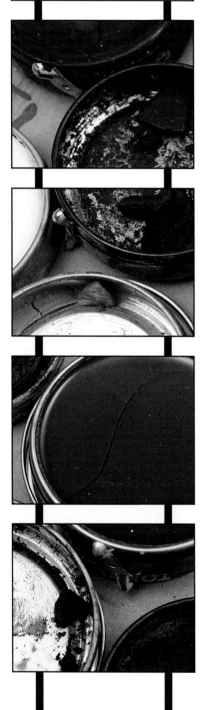

Finishes and sealers

All painted surfaces, including artwork, need to be protected in some way from wear and tear. Some work is enhanced by the addition of a particular finish.

VARNISH

Varnish has become a generic term referring to a general sealer. Polyurethane varnish is mineral spirit-based, and while producing a tough finish, does yellow with age. Water-based varnishes are more popular for interior projects, as they are easier to clean, are relatively odour free, and do not discolour. Both types are available in clear, tinted gloss, semi-gloss, satin or matt (suede) finish.

LACQUER

Not to be confused with shellac, clear lacquer is thinners-based, dries quickly and is highly flammable. It is best to buy this in spray cans to use on small projects. Build up several coats, allowing each to dry between applications. This varnish also has the advantage of not yellowing with age.

TWO-PART VARNISH

This is a polymer-based varnish which comes in a pack containing the varnish and the hardener. Only mix the quantity required in the correct ratio. This varnish is extremely hardwearing and expensive. It can be painted or sprayed onto various surfaces that require a permanent finish.

TWO-PART POLYMER RESIN

Also known as liquid glass, this very expensive sealer forms a tough, protective, clear, high-gloss finish which requires at least two weeks' curing. It is sold in small, equal quantities of sealer and hardener. These must be kept separate. Follow the instructions to the letter. Some brands yellow more than others.

LINSEED OIL

This is pressed from linseeds and is the common base for oil paints. In raw form it is clearer and is used for making artist's colours. Boiled linseed oil dries faster, but yellows with age and is the common base of traditional oil house paint and scumble glaze. (Use on cricket bats and other woods which need to be kept supple, such as granny's rocking chair!)

POLISH AND WAX

These are easily available and economical and form a protective satin finish when applied and buffed. Coloured shoe polishes provide a range of earthy tones, which can be used to stain work as well. Polishes should be applied to porous surfaces and left for a while to be absorbed before buffing to a soft sheen. For a neutral finish it is more economical to use clear floor polish. Liquid furniture wax and liquid shoe polish are less messy to apply, but not as economical.

CRACKLE

Crackle glaze or medium recreates the cracking and crazing of traditional oil-based paints and varnishes which have dried out over time. The glaze is applied between a base and a top coat of water-based paint, resulting in a cracked finish. The glaze shrinks, which forces the topcoat to crack so that the base coat can be seen. It is best to use two contrasting colours for more effect. The number of cracks and how large they are will depend on the thickness of the crackle glaze. The direction of the cracks will depend on the direction of the brushstrokes used in the top layer of paint. For an antique look, use the same colour base and top coats and rub tinted oil-based glaze over and into the cracks. Wipe clean and seal with a polyurethane varnish. It is always best to seal crackle.

There are many types of crackle glaze available, often sold in two parts, but the spray version, while more expensive, is an easy one-step option.

Tools

These vary from the traditional to the obscure. Use your imagination rather than rushing out to buy art supplies.

FINGERS FIRST
These are our most useful appendage – we love to paint with them.

CHARCOAL
Charcoal can be used with great effect, though this can be messy if smudged. It may be fixed with artist's fixative or hairspray.

CHALK
White and coloured chalks work well on dark backgrounds as do China markers. Slivers of dressmaker's chalks work well when drawing fine lines.

PENCILS
For tracing or drawing HB and softer (2B and 4B) are recommended.

PENS
There are so many available! We used permanent markers for most projects.

LINERS
Many acrylic paints are now available in liner bottles. It is cheaper, however, to fill your own, if you can find the appropriate bottle. It is important that the paint is not lumpy, as this will block the liner nozzle. Most liner bottles have plastic nozzles, though there are metal ones available in craft shops, which give a finer line.

Hint: You can use the top metal section on a click pencil as a handy nozzle. Stick this on with masking tape, or screw onto an existing nozzle top. If you can't find liner bottles, use perm-lotion bottles.

SCRATCHERS
Create lines in paint with the backs of your brushes, bamboo skewers, knitting needles, forks, twigs and even long fingernails! Feathers are wonderful for dragging and twirling uneven lines.

BRUSHES
Brushes come in all shapes and sizes and are often use-specific: hake brushes for softening, floggers for dragged effects and so on. For more detail on brushes, why not add a paint manual to your library? Quality varies considerably, though cheap brushes are often good value for money and, if looked after, will last a long time (years!). Raid your local hardware store's special offer bins! For each project we have listed any special brushes used.

Hint: Brushes with bristles that splay, should not be given a haircut with scissors, but rather shaped by "painting" a piece of medium-grit sandpaper, in all directions. Dry brushing bisque-ware also shapes new brushes. A quicker, more drastic way to thin a stiff chunky-bristled brush is to stand the bristles in neat bleach for a minute or two and then neutralize immediately in vinegar. Rinse the brush well and you will find it magically thinned and shaped! This only works on natural bristle and not on nylon. Be careful – you don't want to waste your brush away entirely!

To maintain brushes, always clean them well, in whatever solvent is relevant to the paint used, then wash thoroughly, rinse and dry. The best way to dry brushes is to hang them from the handles, though drying flat will do. Never leave brushes standing on their bristles for long periods, either in the solvent or in a container to dry. This damages the bristles and the brush won't "work" properly with bent bristles. The best way to suspend brushes is by twisting two elastic bands around the handle of the brush and then wrapping them around the tin so that the brush is suspended in the solvent. After washing and drying brushes, squeeze the bristles flat with your fingers and preferably hang from a wire hook.

If used with water-based paint
Rub the brush with a soap bar or green kitchen soap, as it contains no detergent and the fat content bonds with the paint and removes it completely. Rinse well in water. If paint residue has dried in the bristles, scrub with a nailbrush or rub into a plastic scourer pad.

If used with oil-based paint
Use mineral turpentine. Decant into a clean tin or glass jar and rinse the brush in the solvent. Wash as for water-based paint.

Hint: Recycle your turps by allowing the paint residue to settle. Then carefully pour the clean turps into another bottle. Mark as recycled, as it will be slightly discoloured.

If used with solvent-based paint
The process for cleaning is the same as with oil-based paint, but check your paint label carefully and use the correct solvent. Do not try to experiment, as you may find your brush shrivelled to a very interesting shape. If this happens, don't discard the brush; rather frame it or use it for special effects!

ROLLERS
Rollers vary in size, material and use. They absorb more paint than brushes, and therefore require more water for cleaning. We have mostly used sponge rollers for the projects in this book. They are easier to use and keep clean than the fluffy kind, and give the smoothest effect.

Hint: Only use water-based paint with sponge rollers, as solvents will destroy the foam. For oil-based paint use the fluffy or short-pile mohair rollers (make sure these do not have a foam core).

SPONGES

A variety of sponges can be used with water-based paint. For oil-based paint use only natural sponges. Each type will give its own, very different effect; depending on the sponge's texture. Prices vary greatly. Large bath sponges are a cheap option. Triangular sponges on sticks are available from craft shops, as are shaped sponges. High-density sponge, available from foam shops or upholsterers, also works well, as does packing sponge, and can be carved into shapes.

Clean and rinse sponges thoroughly in water. If they get too slimy, add a little cloudy ammonia to water and soak first before rinsing.

Hint: Pick holes in bath sponges for textural effects resembling that of natural (much more expensive) sea sponges.

SCRAPERS

Scrapers include credit-type cards, paint scrapers, palette knives, tile-glue applicators, plastic knives and forks and even hard pieces of card.

OTHER APPLICATORS

Scrunched-up plastic bags, bubble wrap, or other similar materials will give a textural effect when stamped on lightly. Items such as a cork, erasers, absorbent kitchen cloths and so on are also interesting applicators. This list can go on and on, but we do give ideas throughout the projects.

OTHER USEFUL TOOLS

Handy items that we use for nearly all our projects include masking tape, ruler, tape-measure, sandpaper, stencils, stamps, hairdryers, craft knives, cutting mat, scissors and a drill.

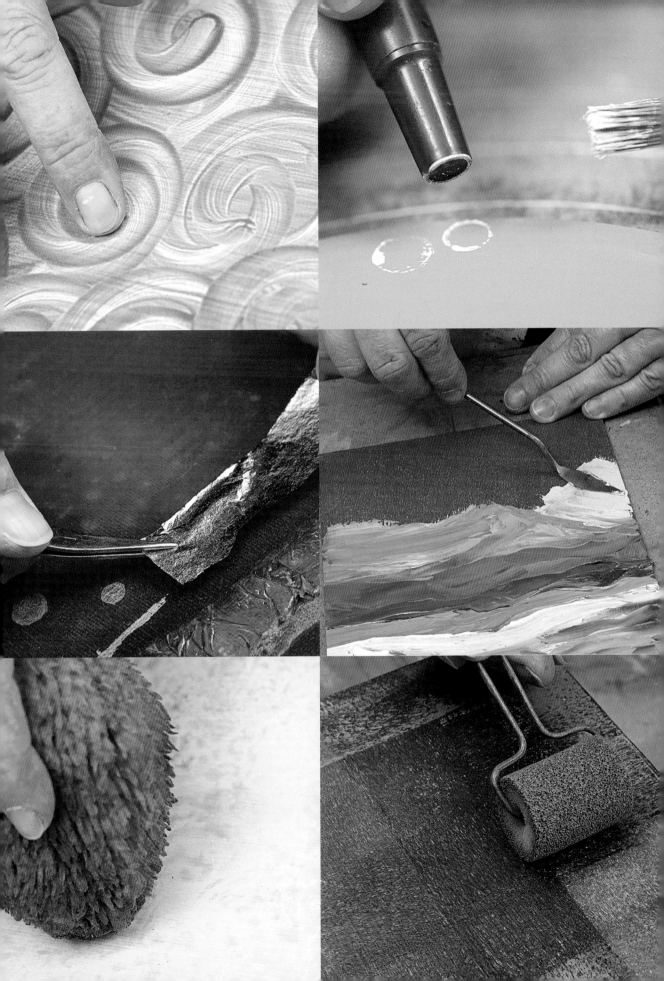

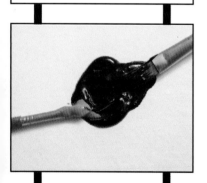

Colour

Using colour is one of the most rewarding and stimulating benefits of any form of painting. We are beginning to know more about how colour affects us emotionally and spiritually. Colour therapy is becoming a developed system of healing, as more is being discovered about how colours can calm, soothe or excite – or even depress – us. Babies and even animals (remember the 'red rag to a bull'!) respond to different colours with different behaviours. Never before have humans had such amazing access to so much colour. We are constantly bombarded with images through digital technology.

In art, more than half the battle is won if your colour combination works well. Visit any hardware or paint shop for an idea of the vast range of colours available.

Hint: Every time you visit a paint shop, help yourself to a few free sample paint swatches to add to your colour library - it's a bit over the top to scrounge the whole range in one go! (Try telling that to a colour-besotted five year old ...)

It is easy to work in colours that we like. However, when we step out of the mould, interesting and creative juices start flowing and our best results are achieved.

Most artists we've talked to have learnt, from books or art classes, to mix their own colours and develop a sense of what works well together – it's not all intuition and serendipity! Control and manipulation have a healthy function in painting – so when you feel the urge to redesign your loved one's habits, channel that energy into vibrant colour and make everyone happy!

Basic colour recipes

The step-by-step process of mixing and painting your own colour wheel is a great way for you to learn about the relationships between colours. There isn't a colour range in the world, however, that always has the right colour, so play around with the wheel, and you'll be amazed at what you can make! Keep your wheel as your most useful colour reference tool.

Primrose, magenta and cyan are the primaries referred to for digital and other printing and fabric painting and dyeing. Below are some basic colour recipes:

HUES

Primary colours	Secondary colours	Tertiary colours
Yellow Magenta red Cyan blue	Orange Green Violet	Amber Red Purple Lime Jade Cobalt

TINTS

Tints are mixed like the hues. By gradually adding white to make pastels, many degrees of tints can be obtained.

SHADES

Shades are mixed like the hues, but with grey or black added in small quantities to tone. The depth of shade will depend on the amount of black added.

EARTH TONES AND NEUTRALS

To bring in earth tones (variations of brown) or neutral colours, we work with mixing complementary colours of each hue. Complementary in this sense means literally the colours which are found opposite each other on the wheel:

Yellow – Violet
Magenta – Green
Blue – Orange
Lime – Purple
Jade – Red
Cobalt – Amber

When deciding which colours will go well with each other in a painting, bear in mind that complementary colours also work well as contrasts. Small quantities of a complementary colour may be mixed with a hue to tone the colour from bright and sharp to muted and earthy, for example magenta with a small amount of green makes maroon. These colours may also be turned into pastels with the addition of white, or toned to shades by adding black or grey.

BROWN

If you mix your primaries in differing ratios, you will get browns ranging from khaki through to milk chocolate to dark chocolate. You may also find the mix becoming grey, even though you didn't use black. Creams and skin tones may be mixed from white and various browns.

USING COLOUR COMBINATIONS

Harmonious colours lie next to each other on the wheel. When deciding on a colour combination, it is always safe to work with triangular patterns, for example, two in harmony spiked with one accent (complementary). Lighter and darker tones of the same colour live in harmony with each other and are comfortable on the eye. More exciting, though, are combinations that make use of a pair of complementary colours such as blue and yellow or orange, or green and red. The warm colours are the magenta/red/orange/yellow half of the colour wheel, while blue/green/purple/violet are the cooler colours. Cool colours are calming and recede, while warmer colours are inviting and exciting.

Primary and secondary pastiche

Having left formal secondary school teaching many years ago to expand my wonderful world of paint and pieces, I am not keen to return to classroom situations. While I was frantically busy with book deadlines and paint projects, however, the plea came from my youngest (and her teacher) to 'baby-sit' her class during their school revue. So to save my sanity amidst the chaos of portable DVD players, electronic and other games (and LOUD noise), I tried to communicate something along the lines of 'Hear no evil, see no evil, speak no evil' (and preferably shut up) but primary school children are not subtle! So I tried to get them drawing and painting and occupy their right brains a little to see if that focused them. It worked very well with the three at a time who were busy working directly on the boards, but the rest just carried on regardless. If anything, the decibel levels rose with the shrieks of derision and critical delight accompanying each minutely scrutinised addition to the boards!

I chose to work with three ready-primed and blocked boards which I had waiting for another project. I explained the concept of primary and secondary colours to the children and told them we'd use each block to explore variations of a primary colour. Primrose Yellow for Ears or listening, Magenta Red for Mouths or speaking and Cyan Blue for Eyes or seeing. As there are 32 in the class I divided each board into 36 blocks. The centre four blocks I painted as one large block in a harmonising secondary colour: orange for the yellow board, violet for the magenta and green for the blue. The children then drew ears, eyes or mouths respectively in wax crayons in the surrounding 32 blocks.

Typically, two didn't listen to the instructions; one drew a mouth and the other an eye very ironically in the middle of the ear (listening) block!

The wax crayons formed an effective resist for the mixture of primary watercolours which I then washed with soft watercolour brushes into each block directly over the drawings. Once dry and varnished with clear lacquer spray, the cheerful, charming results were a happy pastiche of classroom personalities – and turned a dreaded occasion into a fond memory for me!

Before you begin ...

These hints contain some useful information to save you a lot of hassles and the environment from further damage:

- Wear protective clothing and protect your work surface.
- Protect your hands with barrier cream or gloves.
- Sand sharp edges of wooden supports before preparing.
- Cover paint-roller trays with disposable plastic shopping bags, pour in paint, when finished throw away – no mess, no fuss – clean tray.
- Tea break (with Monique these are essential!). Wrap paint-covered brush in a plastic bag – they won't dry out, even after a few hours (or days!).
- Keep toilet paper or kitchen towel handy to clean spills, and to clean excess paint off brushes before immersing in solvents. This saves hugely on solvents.
- Wipe rims of paint tins with paper before closing. This small action saves the frustration of battling to reopen tins. The paint won't dry and cause flaking into clean paint. Dispose of paint and solvent-soiled paper in a dustbin, rather than in the toilet.
- Preferably store paint containers upside down. This prevents a skin forming on the surface.
- Test all colours by painting samples. Your own mixes will differ from shop-bought colours.
- Make sure you have the relevant solvents handy – deal with spills and stains immediately. Don't think 'Oh! I'll come back to this...'
- Always follow the manufacturer's instructions, particularly when using unusual products. (Shhh – We don't always abide by this rule – sometimes it's fun to experiment, just don't blame the manufacturer if it goes wrong – or us!)
- Don't get depressed about messes – they can always be over-painted.

> I begin with an idea and then it becomes something else.
>
> *Pablo Picasso*

P(r)op art door

After many discussions about what would be an appropriate opening project we settled on the obvious: a door! And what good value for money. Cheaper by half than a canvas half its size, this makes an impressive statement and is ready to hang (or prop!)

You will need

Door: 900 x 2000 mm
Wooden panels (we used 9 mm MDF) cut as follows in mm
   10 x 500 x 50   10 x 50 x 100 cm 20 x 100 x 100
   30 x 100 x 150   10 x 100 x 200   1 x 150 x 550
   10 x 150 x 650   10 x 150 x 700   100 mm circle
3 triangles 70 x 70 x 50
crete stone 1-2 kg
Yellow oxide (bum some from a builder friend – about 1 tablespoon)
Sand – sieved gravel and coarse builder's sand
Wood glue
All purpose crack filler
Acrylic texture paste
Credit cards (old!)
Paint brushes
Stanley knife
Cutting board
Old X-ray or plastic sheet
Forks
Combs
Fingers (your own!)
String, map pin and pencil
Glazes: mix 1 part acrylic paint (PVA) in each of the following colours: white, black, blue, green, yellow ochre, orange, red, with two parts water and two parts acrylic scumble glaze
Water-based varnish

Preparation

Use the template on page 120 and draw a semicircle using string tied to a map pin. Mark the panel positions in pencil.

Finishing plaster

1 Mix 1 part wood glue to 2 parts water and add crete stone until it forms a stodgy porridge. Divide mix into two containers and add two teaspoons of yellow ochre

oxide to one container. Use the credit card to smear the mixture onto the door. Working from the outside edge in plain crete stone, add yellow as you progress around the semicircle.

2 Mix left-over crete stone into one container and 1 tablespoon orange paint to tint. Work this mix into the remaining areas thus darkening the edges.

3 Paint wood glue thickly into the semicircle around the marked panel positions and sprinkle with rough-grade sand while still wet (work in sections).

Texture paste panels

1 Use credit card to spread paste onto panels like rough cake icing.

2 On the circle and two smallest squares draw spirals using your little finger!

3 Place one small square into marked texture-pasted panel and set aside to dry.

4 Use triangle to cut triangle stencil in old x-ray or plastic sheet. Place triangle shape in marked position on panel as a block out.

Sand in paint

1 Mix rough builder sand into white PVA. Spread onto marked panels, one small square and two triangles – again use credit card.

2 Carefully lift triangle block-out shape leaving exposed area.

Crack filler

1 Spread remaining panels and triangles as evenly as possible with filler. Comb panels horizontally. Use different widths of comb for each panel.

2 Scrape the triangles from base to apex and place in position on texture-pasted panel. Place positive stencil in position over exposed triangle and slop filler over. Comb carefully and then lift stencil.

3 Use filler and glue to sandwich sand triangles in position. Allow all textured panels to dry thoroughly.

Painting the panels

1 Apply glazes liberally to relevant panels and allow to dry. Add a touch of colour to shade as shown. Recoat if necessary.

2 Paint sides and thin edge around each panel, including raised shapes, with black glaze.

3 Varnish with water-based varnish when dry.

Painting the sand

1 Paint on glazes grading from yellow ochre to deep red as in the picture. Allow to dry and varnish.

Final assembly

Varnish crete stone and, when dry, assemble project with a strong ,multi-purpose adhesive.

Ring the changes

We wanted to paint a black background to the spaces where the coloured panels would be positioned. We ran low on black paint so just outlined each rectangle, stood back and admired the effect (much to our mothers' combined consternation!). Happy accident? You be the judge!

After our mothers' consternation we felt we should perhaps offer a calmer alternative to our original project. We had four strips of MDF cut to fill the spaces. We laid them against each other in the order in which we would place them on the door. They were then plastered with left-over crack filler and we scraped an angular sun shape into them using a credit card. The alternate 'rings' around the sun were built up with the scraped-out crack filler. Before the boards dried, they were separated using a fine blade so as not to damage the design. Shoe polish was applied to the boards when dry and buffed with a soft brush for a final finish. (See shell and fish projects pp 77 and 78 for description.) Our moms were much happier!

Use whichever variation appeals to you – or all of them. Or use the geometric shapes on their own as a work of art.

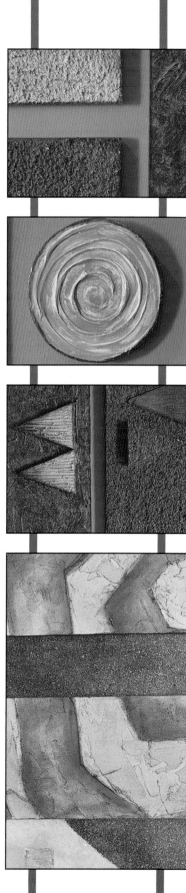

Ab-scratched

We had a little crete stone left from our door project, so rather than waste it we smeared it, using a credit card, onto a spare board that was lurking in the vicinity of our workspace. We added red oxide just to see what it would look like. We needed to try the effect of linseed oil as well, so soon we sloshed some on for good measure and then we waited, and waited … and still it didn't dry. (The cold, wet weather didn't help!) Monique then had great fun scoring and scratching angular lines into the still soggy board with a knife. We added some black oil paint with a brush to emphasize the angles. A few weeks later, the board had faded to a drier finish and Angie added more lines and black to increase the dramatic effect of depth. A truly combined effort!

Work the line

On one of our rare shopping sprees together, we invaded the local art shop and discovered their interesting range of textured, handmade paper. The elephant dung colours inspired us to play – right there on the floor of the art shop. Fortunately the staff and other customers were very tolerantly amused by these two batty females sprawled on the floor. We set out to buy three pieces and came away with eight – enough for each of us to play nicely.

We decided to share a black line and use it in different ways. The addition of a painted brown shadow line adds a three-dimensional quality and draws attention, while the gold leaf adds highlights and an ethereal touch of whimsy to the development of the design. A serendipitous find at the local bead shop produced clever connectors in the form of mini metal clamps for the hanging triptych, with the hanging of extra beads for effect. The whole assembly was suspended from a piece of PVC tube (part of a garden sprinkling system!).

The large sheets of paper were stuck on a bigger backing board, which was painted a mixture of dark brown and black. We used acrylic paints and glue in this project.

> A line is a dot that went
> for a walk.
> *Paul Klee*

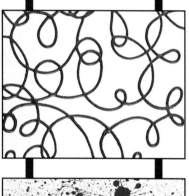

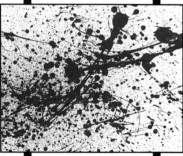

Oodles of doodles

I really like the idea of using things differently from their intended use. Why not revamp old clipboards or use new ones as they offer a very inexpensive way to jazz up any room. I wanted these boards to be quite stark, and based them on doodles – (what else do you do on a clipboard when someone drones on?). Pictured here is Dot, wondering why she was enthusiastically invited into the room and allowed on the bed today with everyone watching!

All the boards were primed with a couple of coats of white PVA (except the black one!). Apart from pen or paint, I wanted to add some texture as well: I did this in the first board (read from right to left) with twine. I couldn't find any in black, so I

painted it with PVA and after it had dried, stuck it onto the board with cold glue, hanging on for dear life, making sure it wouldn't unroll.

The pattern on the black board was painted with puff paint. As puff paint is meant for fabric, which is absorbent, this needed a few coats of the paint for good coverage. I dabbed the paint between coats to get rid of the excess paint also keeping the layers fairly even. I then ironed the board with a hot iron, through a piece of fabric. The paint puffed up, taking on a velvety look and feel (this works really well on fabric). For a more raised effect one would need more layers of paint. If you have puff paint, use white PVA or craft paint.

The third board was splattered with black PVA and a toothbrush. I dipped the brush into the paint and, after removing the excess paint, drew my finger across

the bristles, away from the board. I repeated this a few times until I was happy with the coverage.

Board four was done with texture gel to which I added black craft paint. The gel thickened the paint considerably, allowing me to use it in a liner bottle. I simply made twirls round and round, some of them going off the board. The liner bottle has a tendency to get airlocks and may spatter the gel. If you don't want the trouble – or the texture – a permanent marker could be used.

What fun board five was: I had my children take it in turns sitting still for five minutes (yes, it is possible!). I drew each of them in turn on a piece of paper - but here's the rub – I didn't look at what I was drawing, but kept looking at them (quite disconcerting having your mother stare at you for interminable minutes on end!). I ended up with a family of rather entertaining faces. It was actually quite hard to choose one to use here. A friend suggested giving boards like these to busy moms so that they could be used for relevant notices and so on that seem to mushroom in any household.

The art quotes on board six were written in a thin permanent marker. To get the script straight I ruled lines in pencil and rubbed them out afterwards.

All the boards were finished in a clear lacquer spray.

Mirror art

Spray paint a mirror for a sophisticated teen or a guest shower. Try this project with coloured spray paints for a children's room.

You will need

Mirror
Small mirror mosaics
Clear decorative glass drops
Clear lacquer spray
Super-chrome mirror spray
Dishwashing liquid
Small soft paintbrush
Masking tape
Superglue or epoxy
Lacquer thinners
Glass cleaner

1 Mask off the areas you want to keep free from paint. You may want to paint a complete border or frame – I chose to do one side only as I felt it suited a long, narrow mirror.

2 Paint some large and small spots of dishwashing liquid with the small brush here and there in the design area. This will act as a resist and will result in clear mirror spots in the finished design.

3 Lay the mirror on a flat, level surface so that the paint won't run or drip as you work. Shake the spray paint cans well before you start. Ignore the instructions to hold the can a distance from the work. Start with the clear spray and hold the can a few centimetres perpendicular away from the mirror and give a short sharp burst on the nozzle. The clear lacquer should spurt into a clear, round flat spot of liquid spray-paint resembling a burst bubble surrounded by a misty area of paint. Spray these spots in a random pattern between the detergent spots. Leave space for some super-chrome spots. Spray (at the same close range) the super chrome mirror spots in the gaps.

4 Allow paint to dry thoroughly. The liquid spots will take a little longer than the misted areas so don't be tempted to touch the surface to check. You may spoil the perfect misty or mirror finish and have to start again. When completely dry, peel off the masking tape and use thinners on a small brush to clean off any paint that has bled through the tape. Leave to cure overnight. Wash the mirror carefully with warm water to dissolve the detergent spots. Allow to dry and clean the mirror.

5 Glue mirror mosaic tiles and decorative glass drops in position with superglue for the final touch. Do a trial run, using a little sticky putty to fasten the drops and mosaics to check the effect first. Superglue cannot be removed without risking seven years of very bad luck! (If you aren't superstitious, however, you can al-

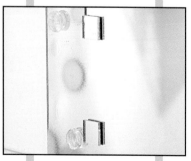

ways turn a broken mirror into a real mosaic artwork for a lifetime of real satisfaction and an heirloom forever! It all depends which way you look in the mirror…)

Hint: If you make mistakes, use the lacquer thinners to wipe the mirror clean and begin again.

Ring the changes

Use beads and ground glass for extra shimmer or recycle using broken coloured rounded glass from old bottles for more interesting and textured mosaic effects. Paint waves in the same way on your bathroom mirror – or fern designs with detergent before spray painting the hallway mirror – the possibilities are as many as you can imagine

Or use your mirror as Da Vinci's advises:
"When you are painting, you should take a flat mirror and often look at your work within it, and it will then be seen in reverse, and will appear to be by the hand of some other master, and you will be better able to judge of its faults than in any other way."

Perspicuous

(Angie wanted to call this pers-plexed as she was amazed at how I did it. But I found this wonderful word which means clear, easily understood and clearly expressed!)

Always on the lookout for inspiration and ideas, (and trying to be ready to recognize them when I see them), I was delighted when I noticed that a section of my worktable would make a wonderful painting – actually there were quite a few bits but I'll keep the others for another day! I wanted to do something a little different with this, so I have painted onto two pieces of identical clear perspex. I had a sheet lying around from another project and my husband (bless his cotton socks – again!) cut it in half and drilled the holes through which they would be connected. Using artists' acrylic I painted, rolled and daubed different shapes and colours onto the two sheets of perspex, deciding what would look better as background and foreground. It wouldn't really have mattered, but I did want the red sun shape to stand out.

My table surface is actually chipboard, and so, if I were true to my source, the backing board to this should have been wood or yellowish. I first thought to break up a piece of chip board for effect, but this seemed like too much work. I then tried sourcing some sawdust, but this was too fine. Nothing quite gelled (and I did want to use something with texture), until Joshua suggested I use wood shavings – the kind you use for hamsters cages. Eureka! (I drew the line at his suggestion of adding a play or stuffed hamster!) When putting the whole thing together, I felt that the wood colour of the shavings overwhelmed the whole thing, as the paint on the perspex is actually quite thin. I painted the board and shavings with white PVA, but in retrospect, spray white would have been easier, not to mention have dried quicker!

The layers are pieced together with long screws, washers and nuts. I needed 'spacers' between the panels to create the three-dimensional look, so Michael kindly cut up one of his old arrows, which did the trick. They are hollow and allow the screws to pass through, while preventing the panels from touching. The heads of the screws add an industrial touch.

Hint: If you do this project, or something similar, it would be best to paint the front panel in reverse, so that the paint is on the underside, which will ensure that it does not get scratched.

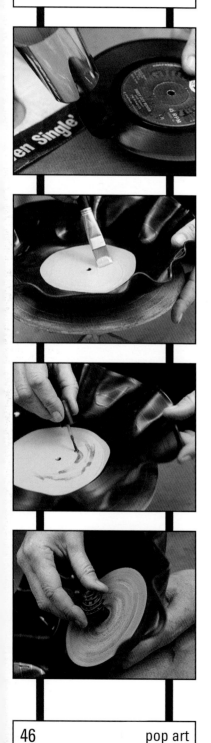

> Design is like the melody, colour the harmony.
>
> *Gautier*

Several spins on pop art

Scratch out those obsolete vinyls you've been hoarding for years and turn them into original arty gifts – but check first you aren't sitting on a collector's item that could make your fortune, like an original Beatles or Elvis recording! If in doubt, there are many websites dedicated to this subject so search the Internet first. For ease of painting, use a turntable – preferably an old one – it just needs to turn, not play music. You can even adapt a potter's wheel for this purpose.

Wavy Day-glo décor

1 Apply heat to your records by using a hairdryer on its hottest setting. Concentrate the heat in one area until the vinyl begins to wilt. Shape it quickly and move the heat on. Continue around the record until you have built a wavy edged bowl, keeping the centre label area flat. (The first one given me was made years ago by a friend's son as a bowl for serving crisps. It wasn't painted and I notice now through the oily deposit that it was an original soundtrack of Woodstock …Thanks, Van Aarde Family!) Warning: if your heat is too fierce – like an oven or heat gun – your vinyl will shrivel before your very eyes and become unusable!

2 Place the clean, wavy record on the turntable and apply paint with a soft brush while the disc is spinning. You can drag lines into the paint by moving the brush sideways as it turns. Beware of exerting too much pressure as resistance may stretch the turntable's drive belt.

3 For these three I used Day-glo pink, green and blue and over-painted the centres in the same way with discarded nail varnish (glitter and sparkle) for a funky effect. Allow to dry and assemble with interesting cupboard door knobs, beads or suitable bling for a teenage girl's room.

Glow in the dark clock

Convert a scratched seven single into a simple wall clock for a boy's room with primer and glow in the dark paint. Spin the primer on in the same way, but allow it to build up in some areas and show the black vinyl through in others. Allow to dry and coat with glow in the dark paint in the same way. Build up at least three coats for a good glow effect (see photograph on page 111). Read *Ah…Tea!* instructions for clock assembly (see page 56). You can paint or stick numbers onto the clock face, but I prefer it plain.

Pretty pancake

The same bright colours used for the wavy decorations were all applied to this flat record. I then placed a paper doyley dead centre and spray painted it with white spay paint and removed the doyley. The colours were softened from Day-glo to pastel by the white spray. A few shiny beads and glass blobs turn this into something a pre-teen girl would love on her bedroom wall.

Colour themes and Mandalas

Experiment with left-over PVA paints and varnishes to create uniquely coloured circles for unusual art pieces suitable for meditation. *Mandala* is another word for *sacred circles*. Mandalas can be used like dream catchers or labyrinths for calming the mind and drawing the viewer into timelessness (some may call it sacred space). It's fun and therapeutic to paint and decorate these. Use paper or foil cut-outs or paint in repeat patterns and borders to enhance these fascinating circles. Mandalas make great gifts too.

Macro montage

This PVA and scumble collage was an exercise in exploring the shapes and colours found in a summer garden – and 'how to use up the leftover dregs of paint from decorating your buildings!'

I threw, painted, dribbled and stamped on ready-primed Masonite squares using all the painting tools I could find to apply the few colours. I was fortunate to be working in the heat of a glass house in a friend's large nursery where I had reference to a vast wealth of beautiful plant forms. They certainly reflect the warmth (and dripping perspiration!) of that time.

Each square works as a little painting on its own, and together they make something endlessly interesting. I stuck Velcro tape onto the back of each one and they can be arranged in a myriad of permutations on a coloured backing board or wall with the corresponding Velcro fasteners

Squares, Madam?
I see no squares!
Piet Mondrian

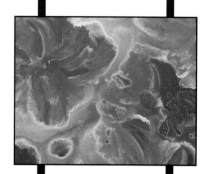

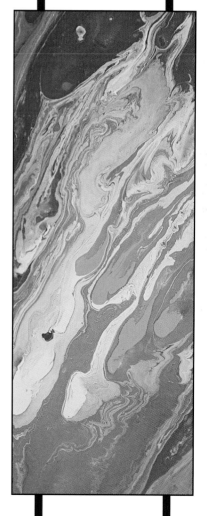

Experimen-tile

These tiles are meant to be decorative, but may be used as wall tiles in dry areas if they are correctly treated and sealed before painting. Otherwise any exposed MDF may swell with damp when stuck to the wall with adhesive and grout.

You will need

As many tiles as you need: I used 70 mm x 70 mm x 3 mm MDF off-cuts ready primed
Glass paint (solvent-based): white, frosted, blue and purple
Gold or silver metallic powder
Denatured alcohol (methylated spirits)
Paint brushes for each colour
Droppers or liner bottles
Thinners for cleaning
Resin or liquid glass (two-part polymer – used by decoupeurs)

1 Coat the sides and top of each tile with single colours of glass paints. Paint rings or drop blobs in a contrasting colour onto the still wet painted tiles.

2 Quickly drop alcohol followed by a little water from liner bottles onto the wet glass paints in a random way. Watch while the paints move and blend into fascinating patterns. Encourage them into swirls with a toothpick or spoon handle. Add a little more alcohol if needed – add thinners too, just to see the effect as it thins the paints if they start drying too quickly.

3 Drop, sprinkle or puff a little gold powder sparingly onto each tile if desired. Allow to dry. This will take at least a few hours. Be patient and don't touch the surface, as it will spoil. The surface of the dry tiles will look a little dull and uneven or pitted in places.

4 Apply resin or liquid glass to each tile for a perfect gloss surface which imitates glass/ceramic or enamel and gives life and depth to the painted design. Read the resin instructions very carefully and follow to the letter. These usually require mixing the two resin parts equally, then pouring it onto the tiles and encouraging it right up to the edges with an ice-cream stick or other disposable tool. Resin needs to be worked quickly (it starts drying after 15 minutes) and in a very clean area. Protect your drying tiles from dust or dirt which could ruin the high-gloss finish. Again, do NOT be tempted to remove the dust cover or peek at your tiles for at least 24 hours. The tiles will then require a further two weeks to harden and cure completely.

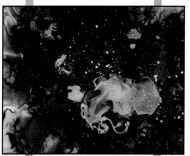

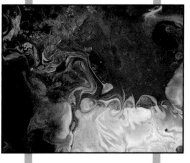

Acciden-tile!

The little tiles on this tray were my first experiments when I used a mixture of oil and alcohol-based paints. Unfortunately they were discoloured by the polymer varnish and I almost discarded them in disappointment. Sarie found this delightful little tray at a second hand shop and reassured me that my tiles looked antique and therefore just perfect with it.

Daisy chain

Even the simplest of motifs can be made more interesting by adding texture - probably one of the main ingredients, besides colour, of any successful work.

Stencils are a great tool when you don't feel like (or can't) draw. I have used a small daisy stencil here as well as a (three-part) larger one: I first painted my board a pale stone colour. The large daisy negative was then placed as a block out, only half on the board. A darker stone colour was used to paint around this block out, creating a darker background and lighter daisy. Sand and glue was mixed into white and blue PVA, adding texture, which were stencilled into the petal and centre sections of the large daisy respectively. The smaller daisies were filled in using crack filler to create a raised effect. Highlights of pale blue were then dry-brushed over the raised daisies. I took care not to get any of this blue onto the stone background, as it would have spoiled the effect. The templates are on p 121.

The templates are on p 121.

> I just let my brain rest when I paint flowers.
> *Renoir*

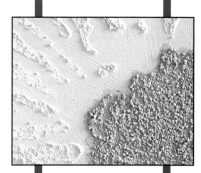

Ah ... tea!

My dear, life-long partner in paint is an addict ... and not just to pop-art. Yup – you've guessed it – she marks the hours in cuppas. After all these years I still find it a trifle disconcerting, while in the midst of intense concentration on artwork or writing, to have my peace time disrupted with loud bleatings of 'Tea! Now!'

Maybe my metabolism is the problem, but I just can't cope with hourly tea breaks (she has her hubby and children as well-trained waitrons too, I might add), so as a tongue-in-cheek tribute to this years' birthday and this book; I made Monique her very own cuppa clock. Tea-time pieces and peace times! No hours are marked – all hours on this baby are Tea-time!

As a paint exercise, the point was to try out the effect of different varnishes on different paints. I combined the clock with the boards and tiles and vinyl poppies as a bright red kitchen theme. The white, brown and black colours fit well into the conventional white-tiled kitchen with wooden cupboards and black and steel appliances. Use your own combinations – try blue poppies with lime centres, for example.

You will need

Melamine bowl and dinner plate (recycle or buy from supermarket)
Plastic battery-operated kitchen clock with black hands
Narrow plastic strip for handle (I used an old paint-bucket handle)
Sand paper
Appliance white spray paint
Circular disc cut from card to fit inside rim of bowl
Acrylic paint in terracotta, brown and white
Medium artist's brush
Pen lids and empty ball point refill for stamping
Two-part epoxy resin or liquid glass varnish
Sticky putty
Hot glue gun

1 Sand the bowl and plate well before spraying with appliance white. Apply at least three coats for good cover resembling a porcelain shine (allow to dry well between coats). Sand and spray the plastic handle as well.
2 Paint the circular disc with tones of terracotta and brown to resemble tea – check your own cuppa for colour matching! Add brown for a rim shadow and paint in white highlights. (If you are a dinosaur like me and still have a record turntable, punch a hole in the centre of the disc and apply the paint with a brush carefully while the disc is turning for a truly effective stirred cuppa look! I cheated and used a discarded computer CD covered with a piece of card. Shop for the right-sized bowl to fit!) Stamp tiny white surface 'bubble rings' on your 'tea', using the pen lids

and round open end of the refill for really minute bubbles. I arranged my bubbles around the edge in quarter spaces so that they mark time … sort of.

3 Mix a small quantity of two-part epoxy varnish (liquid glass) and apply to the painted tea surface. Encourage the varnish to flow right up to the rim. Place under a dust cover until cured.

4 Take apart the clock by pulling off the hands and removing the works from the back of the clock. This is usually stuck on with double-sided tape in the cheaper clocks, so prise it off with a blunt knife. Stick the clock works with the hot glue gun onto the back of your tea disc. The clock spindle must fit through the centre on the painted tea side. Replace the hands onto the spindle in the order of hour, minute and second. Add a battery and check that your clock ticks!

5 Attach the clock disc to the inside of the bowl with sticky putty, so that the rim of the disc rests against the sides of the bowl. You can then remove it when the battery needs replacing. Glue the plastic handle to the side of the bowl. Glue the bowl to the plate. And there you have it … a really large, flattened yet three-dimensional painted cuppa! (My family thought it was a weird plate of soup until it was wall mounted – they're always shaking their heads at my crazy ideas). I mounted the clock on a red backing board for contrast.

Red faux-lacquer backing board

Real lacquer consists of many layers of liquid shellac painstakingly applied, drying well between each coat and building up to a deep shine. For the bright translucent high-gloss textured sheen of this board, I cheated by painting it with flat red PVA and varnished it with yellow solvent-based glass paint which I diluted 1 part paint to 3 parts acetone. I applied the varnish in two coats criss-cross. It dried really quickly and gave the red a wonderful brilliance, left brush strokes for texture and faked the depth of real lacquer.

Pop(py) art

I have access to a huge collection of old pop music seven singles, picked up for a song by my dear friend Sarie Marais (really, truly) who snuffles around the second-hand shops in search of special items to sell in aid of Cat Care's sterilization sponsorship programme. So I'm able to experiment widely with them, knowing I am doing my bit for feline health care. These ones were shaped by plunging them into a bowl of boiling water. Wearing rubber gloves I was able to bend the edges into petal curves similar to that of poppies. As vinyl cools, it hardens. I re-dipped often to soften and re-work the plastic until I was satisfied.

I painted the 'poppies' in plain red PVA with black centres and, when dry, varnished them with clear gloss lacquer spray. The centres were created from wooden beads and artificial stamens found at a florist supplier. If you can't get them, substitute with black sewing thread dipped repeatedly in varnish and allowed to dry until stiff and bendable. I attached them with silver wire through the centre hole of the bead to the record and glued the poppies to a white backing board with the glue gun.

White backing boards

Both white boards are the same size as the red one and were painted with white PVA. I varnished one with clear matt glaze-coat as a background for the shiny poppies. The other was sealed with semi-gloss clear water-based varnish for a soft sheen to show off the tiles.

Tiles

These were done the same way as those in the experimen-tile project (see page 52), except that I used a combination of water, oil and solvent-based paints to create them. I deliberately didn't varnish them, as I liked the resulting textured, shiny and matt effects.

Now Monique just has to re-paint and accessorize her kitchen to match her tea-time-piece…

Mosaic miscellany

I found these mosaics while looking for something entirely different and loved the metallic veins and the contrast between the matt and shiny mosaics. I just had to do something with them. I wanted to keep to the geometric theme, so I used them in conjunction with the mesh, creating interesting textures in the texture paste.

You will need

2 ready-made canvases about the size of an A3 piece of paper
High-solid texture paste
Palette knife (credit card or spatula will also do)
Mesh
Mosaics
Small tube of burnt umber oil paint
Small amount of linseed oil
Lint-free cloth
Glue

1 Cover one canvas all over with the texture paste. This doesn't have to be too thick. Just make sure that the canvas is properly covered. Cover with a piece of mesh and smooth down, removing the excess paste as you go. When the mesh is lying flat, remove it carefully, creating an impressed mesh pattern in the paste.
2 Carefully push the block of mosaics into the centre of the canvas. Place the matt mosaics into place along the side. Leave to dry.
3 Cover the second canvas in the same way with texture paste, impressing a smaller rectangle of mesh into the centre and leave in place. Add more texture paste around the edge of the mesh, creating a thicker, uneven texture. Impress two more rows of the matt mosaics, lining up with those on the first canvas. Add four mosaics on the bottom right, making a small square. Leave to dry thoroughly.

4 Glue the remaining mosaics in place on top of the mesh. Allow the glue to dry.
5 Rub a small amount of raw umber oil paint on each corner of the first canvas, working in with your finger or a soft, lint-free cloth. You can help it to spread with a little linseed oil. Also rub the raw umber around the mosaics, creating an uneven aged effect. Keep adding raw umber, until you are satisfied that your canvases are dark enough. Shade the second canvas in the same way. The sides of the canvas are shaded in the same way
6 Leave to dry. The oil paint may take quite a while to dry, depending on how much you have used.

Leafscape

This is a great project to learn lots about texture and colour. We did it together, and four hands and two very subjective opinions proved to be really useful! These instructions are based on how we worked. Using your own design and combination of textures, you can create something similar, but different. While our textures make a picture, they could have been affixed to the wall or a backing board with Velcro, enabling the panels to be shifted around to make many abstract permutations – try a different one every week and see if your neighbours notice!

You will need

20 boards 300 x 300 mm
White all-purpose primer
PVA paint in light blue, teal blue, dark blue, green, yellow, cream, orange, red, brown, black
Water-based acrylic scumble glaze
Water-based clear matt or suede varnish
Polyurethane varnish (optional – recommended for outdoors)
Methylated spirits
Spray bottle with water
Brushes: various wall brushes, including flogger (very long bristles)
Teaspoons and containers for mixing paint (polystyrene flat punnets)
Masking tape
Bucket of clean water and towel
Paper towel
Texture tools: Roller; leaf stamp; scrap paper; plastic bags; sponge; mutton cloth; cling wrap; graining comb; dropper; sticky putty

Preparation

Give the boards a coat of primer, using a roller. When dry, paint with a base coat of cream PVA. Mix and label glazes for each colour in the following proportions: 1 part PVA to 2 parts scumble and 2 parts water. In more humid areas use less water and scumble (1,5 parts). Mix two blues and 10 greens from three blues, yellow and orange. Tone the greens, using yellow, orange, red and black to create natural shades. Place the boards side by side on a large work area: five across and four down, creating a large patchwork rectangle. Draw the design lightly in pencil onto the prepared boards. Remove errors and dirty marks carefully with abrasive cleaner.

Hint: Keep the boards together by laying them onto strips of masking tape, sticky side up.

	1	2	3	4	5
A					
B					
C					
D					

Paint the sky

1 Start in the lightest area of sky (row B, column 2): brush the boards across row B horizontally with water, following the lines of the design. Now brush on light blue glaze. We had fun sweeping the brush across the wet sky area, moving our bodies as though we were in dance class! Our long brushstrokes inevitably crossed the pencil lines – so we tidied this a little later with damp paper towel.

2 While the glaze is still wet, carefully lift row B out and place on a separate working surface. Spray B2 with water, aiming more towards the bottom of the 'V'. Carefully place back in position.

3 Add water to right side of B1 with a brush. Lift and allow to drip horizontally to the left. Tilt the board until you are satisfied with effect and place back in position.

4 Use a brush and flick meths across the wet paint on boards B3-5. Allow enough drying time (they will take longer to dry than the plain glaze) and place back in position. Now continue dragging light blue glaze across row A, adding darker blue about half way up, blending the two.

5 Smudge a cloud in A1 using your hand, and soften with the flogging brush. Add extra dark glaze at the top of A4 and A5. Flog across the top of Row A, blending the blues from light to dark.

Paint the lighter land/leaf

1 Starting in the top section, follow the line of the pattern and brush on a light green glaze. Add a slightly darker green as you progress downwards. Fill the entire section in this way.

2 Starting in the tip of the leaf shape (C1 and C2), randomly stamp off the glaze using the leaf stamp. Clean the stamp on a piece of scrap paper.

3 Texture B3 and C3, using a small dry brush, twirled in the glaze for a circular effect.

4 Comb B4 and C4, also in a curved fashion.

5 Stamp off B5 and C5 with a twisted lump of sticky putty. Use darker greens in the bottom of the leaf section.

6 Texture C1 and C2 by stamping on to the area in two lighter greens, using the leaf stamp. Use a sea sponge and two medium greens to create the texture on C3.

7 "Bag" C4 and "rag" C5 using the deeper greens. Simply dip a scrunched or twirled plastic bag and rag respectively into the glaze and twist onto the surfaces.

8 Using the deeper green glazes, and keeping within the design area, paint D3 to 5. Now sponge off the glaze on D3, creating a subtly different texture to C3. Bag and rag off D4 and D5 respectively. Paint the centre line green and streak it carefully with two fingers.

Paint the darker land/leaf

Paint two darker green glazes, mixing the two as you go. "Massage" the glaze with three fingers in a circular motion to texture B1 and D1. (This took us back to our pre-school years!) C1 is textured in much the same way using one finger to make more definite spirals. Give B2, C2 and D2 an interesting "malachite" texture with a brush.

Paint the base ground

1 Colour-wash D1 to D3 with olive and darkest green glazes. We used wavy brush-strokes, leaving lovely lines in the glaze. Drop (rather than paint), glazes on D4 and D5. Dab clingwrap into D1 and crumpled paper into D2.

2 Dapple the remaining three boards with meths from a dropper – more intensely on D4 and D5. This is great fun to watch developing but bear in mind that it will take ages to dry.

Finishing off

Allow all the boards to dry completely and sponge on one coat of water-based varnish. Allow to dry and work over areas that need more colour. To do this effectively first apply a coat of scumble glaze to the relevant areas. Coloured glaze can be added and adjusted easily without affecting the original work. When we were finally satisfied, we left it to dry and had several satisfying cups of coffee before settling down to write this up!

Coat with polyurethane varnish if your artwork is for outdoors use.

Earthscape

This painting is a very simple landscape with few lines to draw. Cement-based paints, crack filler, rust paint and the solid painted backing it fits onto, lifts it out of the ordinary. Cement paints usually dry within half an hour, so you won't even have time for tea in between painting sky and mountains!

You will need

Backing board pre-primed and large enough to fit
3 identical Masonite pre-primed squares
Pencil
Crack filler – ready-mixed
Cement-based paints in blues, greys, white and terracotta (mix each well with 1 part wood glue to 6 parts paint to improve adhesion)
Rust paint
Glaze coat in clear matt finish
Plastic knife, fork and spoon and credit card or scraper
Paint brushes – small oil and large wall
Staple gun or small nails and hammer

1 Place the three squares face down abutting in a horizontal line. Stick together with long strips of masking tape and turn them over to the right side. Draw the landscape across them in pencil (template on page 124). Spoon and spread crack filler into the design lines and scrape and paste the filler into the landscape. Flatten the paste in the further hills and mountains and roughen the texture with the fork and spoon handle in the closer foothills and plains. Allow to dry overnight.
2 Drag the blue and grey cement paints horizontally across the top half of the boards. Add a streak of white here and there into the wet paint and re-drag, blending the 'clouds' into the sky. It doesn't matter if you drag paint over the paste textured mountains. They will be covered later. Allow to dry.
3 Drag a little of the terracotta colour across the bottom half of the boards. Leave some of the land area the natural colour of the crack filler and dry-brush some terracotta and grey over it. Allow to dry. Drag the backing board and its sides in similar fashion: top half predominantly grey and blue and bottom half terracotta. The cement paint will leave its own textural streaks as it dries.
4 Paint the hills and mountains in rust oxide, dark undercoat or metal primer, depending on the rust paint you are using. Paint the edges of the boards to correspond with the colours used across the surface. Paint the rust paint over the mountains where you want them to be coloured lighter and immediately brush on the rusting agent and wait for the rust colours to develop. If you want some areas to remain darker than others, dilute the rust agent with water or apply less.
5 Remove the masking tape holding the boards together when they are completely dry. Seal the backing board with two coats of glaze coat. Assemble your painting

by aligning the three boards across the backing board and staple or tack them in place. Dot the staple/nail heads with a tiny dab of the relevant colour paint to hide them. Hang your painting where you will have space to gaze 'through' its window into desert space. Grab a cuppa, put your feet up and relax into your new view.

Patter-splatter

This is a more sophisticated take on the handprints all pre-schoolers take home as mementos of their handiwork for posterity, and came about by chance. I was messing with purple paint and couldn't find a rag to clean my hands so that my already bespattered telephone wouldn't be completely ruined when I answered its incessant bleating! I quickly patted them onto a board to get the worst off. I rather liked the effect it left and so, rather than cleaning the board, I experimented with it to a further degree. I continued patting in a similar direction onto three identical sized boards; one was already painted lavender while the other two were white. I got my hands covered in paint all over again with the cerise, terracotta and lavender PVA colours I happened to be working with at the time – and just hoped the phone wouldn't ring again!

The final effect needed brightening and some contrast of texture, so I dribbled bright solid white and cerise off a paint stirring stick across the three abutting boards. Voila!

Hint: Before using your hands as a painting tool, rub them well with aqueous cream as a paint barrier. Make sure you get lots of cream under your nails, as paint is difficult and even painful to remove when dry. There are some very expensive 'silicone glove' creams available, but the cheap stuff also works quite well.

Make waves – and hang ten!

These two simple monochromes are painted as one item and then separated. All you need is two ready-primed painting blocks. Place them abutting side by side. Use 1 part PVA (in a suitable colour) diluted to a thin glaze with 2 parts water and 2 parts water-based scumble glaze. Sweep this in a wave across the two boards. Cover the entire surface and blocked sides of the boards with glaze in the same wave-like pattern. While this is still wet, fill a small liner bottle with some white spirits or methylated spirits or turpentine and drop along the wave line and allow the bubble foam effect to develop. This is basically the same effect as 'cissing' – and it's as easy as that. You can make ten in an afternoon when the waves are too flat to surf!

Varnish the finished boards with water-based varnish if spirits was used, poly-urethane if turps was used.

Mount on a backing board painted in the same colour of the glaze, but in solid PVA for a dramatic frame.

> You can't stop the waves, but you can learn to surf.
>
> *Jon Kabat-Zinn*

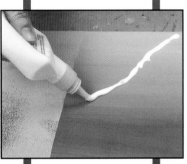

Sandy bay

Who could live near the sea and not want to paint it some time or another? I wanted to keep this really simple, capturing the idea of waves dancing in the sun.

You will need

5 boards (measured in mm)
  1 x 400 x 400
  2 x 400 x 100
  2 x 400 x 200
  (The centre panel could stand on its own if you don't want such a wide piece)
Paint: PVA in grey blue, stone, white; white enamel
Brushes
Roller
Containers for paint
Masking tape
Fine builder's sand or sea sand
Cold glue

1 Prime the boards with white PVA – I gave mine two coats. Place the boards side by side, with the square in the middle, the two narrow panels on either side and then the medium panels on the outside. Add tape on the underside to keep them together. The panels are painted as if they were one: Starting with white PVA across the top, blend with a small amount of blue, getting darker towards the bottom. No need to go all the way down as the bottom half gets a slightly different treatment. When blending, keep your brushstrokes long, going from one edge to the other.

2 Allow to dry thoroughly. Move the narrow panels up by about 1 cm and the medium panels up by about 2 cm. Measure just less than half way up on the square panel and put a length of masking tape across all five boards at that point. Make sure that the edge is flat against the board. Paint in the blue across the panel, adding a little stone as you go, shading with long brushstrokes as before.

3 Remove the tape gently and allow the paint to dry. With a wide roller or brush, paint a thick stripe of stone, slightly off-centre, on the square panel. You do not want this to block out the background completely, so be gentle.

4 Allow to dry and paint some cold glue where you want the sand to go. Sprinkle sand into the wet glue. Lift the panels gently to remove the excess sand. Dribble some white enamel alongside the sand and leave to dry. This will take a few days, depending on the weather.

Simply sea (e)scape

Many years of beach-walking at dawn inspired this painting. I needed to fill a blank wall above my bed and what better than my favourite subject and suitable colours. Work from a photograph if you don't have the sea on your doorstep. And even if you do, photographs are a very useful memory aid and guide for colour and general shape and proportion when working from home. A painting this size cannot be attempted on the beach anyway!

I took this photograph on the day I was lucky enough to swim with wild dolphins in the waves. Somehow I had to capture that incredible memory. I omitted the dolphins as they are only dots in the photo and I could not do justice to them in mere paint.

With computer manipulation you can turn even the poorest grade photograph into useful inspiration by cropping out unwanted bits and changing the hue for a more pleasing effect. The simple horizontal lines of this picture eliminate the need for a formal drawing or design. The lines naturally draw the eye into endless reflective space creating a serene mood.

You will need

Blocked primed board: height measurement a third of the width
Paint: PVA in white, orange, blue and green (small tubs of green and blue craft acrylic will be sufficient)
Copper paint and Verdigris agent (optional – I used it because I had some left over from another project)
Clear gloss varnish (water-based or polyurethane)
Texture paste or gel medium
Beach or fine builder's sand
Wide wall-painting brush (or wallpaper-paste brush)
Medium oil-painting brush
Wide masking tape
Plastic spoon

1 Mix some orange PVA with white to a softer hue. Drag this colour across the entire board horizontally. I inherited an old wallpaper-paste brush which is so easy to use. Three side swipes and I was done! While paint is still wet, add plain orange to the top edge of the board and re drag blending the colour again horizontally so that it deepens the 'sky' part of the painting. Add a few streaks of orange further down towards the centre of the painting and blend these in the same way. Allow to dry thoroughly.

2 Take two pieces of wide masking tape, longer than the width of the board, and 'low-tack' them by pressing onto a fabric surface first before using. The glue is so strong on masking tape it can pull up the freshly dried PVA underneath if you omit this step. Lightly mask a horizontal line a little below halfway down your board.

Measure both sides evenly so that your horizon doesn't slant. (You wouldn't want to feel seasick in bed!) It doesn't matter if the paint seeps under the masking tape, as this will add to the sea effect. The masking tape is merely a guideline. Mask a second line two thirds parallel below the first.

3 Mix a few spoons of texture paste or gel with blue acrylic paint and a little water to a soft, buttery consistency and add a touch of the orange to tone it to teal. Paint this across the top half of the masked area. Drag and twirl the oil-painting brush in uneven parallel lines, making sure you leave some of the background colour showing though the waves as small horizontal streaks. This will 'reflect' the sky colour on the waves. Divide the blue gel mix into two small tubs. Mix green paint into one blue gel mix, adding a little orange and white to create a sage grey-green. Paint this mix in the same way into the lower half of the area, between the masked lines.

4 Lift the masking tape. Repaint the sea with more of the two gel mixes, leaving horizontal textured waves. Introduce a little of the sage green into the deeper ocean area and vice versa. The sculpted texture will dry much flatter than it appears at this stage.

5 Mix a few spoons of white PVA with texture gel and some sand. Dab a little here and there for foamy waves. Use the bowl of the spoon and twirl the brush to 'scoop' the foam into horizontal wave-like froth. Go easy on this, or you will end up with a wild, stormy mess! Flatten the foam on the sand end of the sea; create more texture and wider rolling foam effects here and there for breaking waves; and add a very few thin lines towards the sea horizon creating the illusion of receding perspective. Analyse your sea photograph critically. Examine the relative widths and placements of white foam and, while not slavishly copying their exact looks and positions, do try to imitate their overall effect.

6 If using, streak copper paint lightly with a dry brush onto the sandy beach area. Paint on a little verdigris agent and allow to develop. If not using copper paint, mix a thin glaze of sage green with some varnish and streak that gently instead to simulate wet sand reflecting sky.

7 When dry varnish the sandy beach with gloss varnish to give it that wet look. Allow to dry and contemplate. If your sea is too dark and gloomy, add a more little sky colour in horizontal streaks on top of the water colours. The sea can also be made to look more 'wet' by streaking varnish here and there for effect but go easy on this as it will diminish the effect of the wet beach against a more textured ocean.

Now lie back and imagine the dolphins surfing the waves!

Computer manipulation of photograph

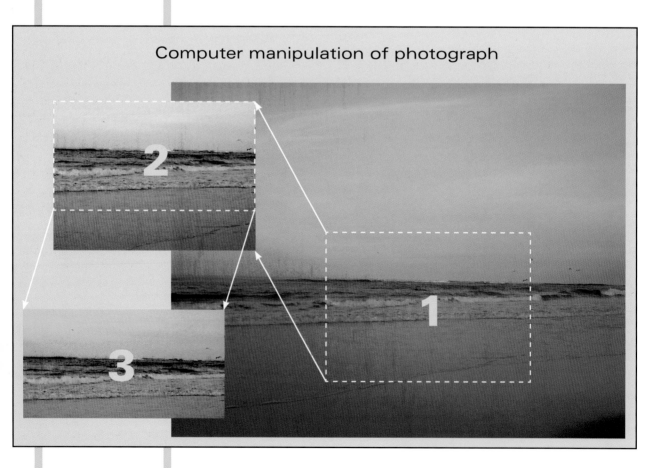

4²?

Initially inspired by the wonderful colours in the square mosaics, I became a little carried away with all the colours, textures and different material possibilities. I spent a huge amount of time deliberating on the possibilities and options. Joshua was in the throes of a major "scoobiedoo" obsession, so I just had to include a circle made by him – in the right colours of course! The triangle is made up of odd shaped beads and the diamond is a fizzy drink can which I have cut into strips and woven together – It's all in the colour!

Each of the backgrounds are textured by impressing different things into texture paste which had first been smoothed onto the boards: The "square" square has a background textured with mesh. The circle is textured with bubble wrap and the diamond with a wider mesh – the type used in the garden. The triangles were a little trickier: I eventually made a strip using cardboard and sponge cut-outs in the triangle shape, which I impressed one row at a time.

The backgrounds were all textured first, adding the centre detail while the texture paste was still wet, adding extra paste where needed to secure the detail.

When each square was dry, I used oil paints in blue and purple to add jewel colours to the texture paste. I dabbed it on with a brush, helping it along with a little linseed oil. I rubbed it in and blended it with a cloth. It needed a few layers before I was entirely happy.

The final finishing touch was to put the squares into frames (a frame makes all the difference). I couldn't find the right colour (that word again!), so I had pine frames made and painted them in navy. I dry-brushed them with silver craft paint, softening the effect and making them more lustrous.

You could enshrine small treasured items in this way, making small 'icons' of them instead of leaving them lurking inside your bottom drawer.

Sea shells on the sea shore

I didn't want to use texture paste for these shells, as it has a tendency to shrink, so I decided to use crack filler. There are quite a few types on the market under various names, some better known than others. On visiting my local hardware store on a reconnaissance mission my husband was sidetracked by drills and timers, so I asked the assistant for help choosing the right crack filler for what I had in mind. He looked at me funny and called for backup. Both chaps then stood there scratching their heads. I experimented anyway and eventually used the "flexible" type for these sea shells. Asking for help is sometimes hazardous, but often worth the entertainment!

You will need

4 boards (hardboard or super wood), blocked
250 ml crack filler (mixed) per board
Wood glue: 25 ml per 250 ml crack filler
Scraper or old credit card
Skewer or other pointed instrument
Sandpaper
Fork
Paint: PVA in white, pale grey blue, stone
Varnish
Paint brushes
Spray bottle

1 Sand the boards lightly to roughen. Mix the crack filler very well so that there are no lumps. It should be a creamy consistency. Coat the entire board evenly with crack filler, using your scraper.

2 Draw the outline of the shell with the skewer (see templates on page 122). If it doesn't look right, cover your marks and redo. If the filler feels too dry and is not that malleable, you can spray with a little water, but don't make it too wet. Once you are satisfied with your drawing, scrape away the areas in the shells that have holes, such as the pansy shell and the sea urchin. Now scrape across the shells, following their natural curve. Create a smooth or a rough texture, depending on how hard you press, and how much of the filler you remove while scraping. If you remove too much filler, you can always add some back. Spray lightly with water if the filler becomes too dry to work with.

3 When you are happy with the scraping, add the textural detail to those shells that need it: The pansy shell's detail was made by drawing in the ovals with the skewer and creating a swirled pattern. The striped edges of the ovals were made by pushing a fork into the filler down each side. The texture in the sea urchin was made with a textured massage roller. The more three-dimensional dots were made by adding a lump of filler and twirling with a skewer.

4 Allow the filler to dry overnight, then paint the edges of the blocks with white PVA to prime them.

5 The same painting method is used for all the shells. Start by painting the blue in the background area (corners). While this is wet you can add a little stone colour and blend in, so that the area is not 'flat'. Paint in the 'holes' in the same way.

6 Paint the blue along the edges of the shell and while still wet, add stone and blend with the blue, then add white, also blending this in. The shell should appear lighter in the raised areas. PVA dries quickly, so if you are not happy with your painting, wait for it to dry and start again. When you are happy, wait for the paint to dry and dry-brush white over the shell, so highlighting the raised areas.

7 Paint the stone or blue, or mixture of the two around the block. Allow to dry and varnish.

Cera-mimic shells

An interesting alternative is to spoon crack filler mix within the lines of the design and to use plastic cutlery to spread the filler carefully to the edges of the shell. Sculpt the shell shape, building it thicker and thinner and scraping out lines within the design. Wet the paintbrush and use it as a modelling tool also, to soften edges and sweep lines smoothly. When you are satisfied with your shell, dip the wet paintbrush into the filler paste and 'paint' diluted filler into the background of the shell right up to the edges of the board. Create swirls or lines of texture with the 'filler-water paint' and allow to dry until hard.

These shells are not painted, but are coloured with polish. Decide which parts of the shell are to be left light and cover these with a little clear wax floor-polish using a toothbrush. Spread coloured shoe polish onto the rest of the shell (navy, military tan and toney red). Use navy polish on the background (if you prefer a lighter blue, cover the background with the clear floor-polish first) and the other colours as shown in the photographs. Leave this to set for at least 15 minutes and then buff shells with a shoe brush – start from the centre of the shell and work outwards. This takes some elbow grease, so get your energetic child to take a turn. If your shoe and tooth brushes get clogged with too much polish, the colours will turn muddy. Rub them well into a bar of kitchen soap and scrub with a nail brush in hot water to dissolve the wax. Dry the brushes well with an old towel before reusing.

If needed, add clear polish to lighten and darker polish to create shadows or deepen colours. Again allow polish to set before brushing off thoroughly. Leave the shells to set for about an hour and then smear the boards gently and generously with clear floor polish (or use your hands or an old rag) before buffing vigorously to a beautiful sheen with a clean, soft cloth. Templates on page 122.

> One is free, like the hermit crab, to change one's shell
> *Anne Morrow Lindbergh*

Fantastical fish fossil

Fish out some of your live-in handyman's flexible crack filler and surprise him with a 'fossil' to hang in the bar or at the braai. Make it as big as that fantastic one that got away!

> Never forget that only dead fish swim with the stream!
>
> *Malcolm Muggeridge*

You will need

Fish design – I used a barracuda (snoek)
Board to fit design (old or battered boards will add even more character)
Ready-mixed flexible crack filler (quantity will depend on the size of your fish)
Exterior crack filler/plaster mix and crete stone
Shellac flakes and some very small shells
Small piece of ribbed washing machine or other plastic hose
Wood glue
Shoe polish (I used neutral, grey and black)
Artist's palette knife
Bamboo skewer
Plastic knife, fork and spoon and old credit card
Small, stiff paintbrush (oil-painting type)
Old toothbrushes and shoe brushes
Soft cloth for buffing

1 Trace fish design on page 124 onto board. (Chalk the back of the design and then trace the lines firmly with ballpoint pen to transfer a chalk outline to the board. Redraw the outlines on the board with 2B pencil). Mix 6 parts crack filler with 1 part wood glue. Spread glue-filler paste thinly into the fish shape using the plastic knife or credit card. You should be able to make out the fish design lines through the paste. Use the serrated edge of the knife or the blade of the palette knife to scrape the fine lines of the fins in the paste.

2 Flesh out the body slightly from the fins by adding a little more paste with the back of the knife blade. With the spoon, work scales from the tail fin to the gill over the top half of the fish's 'streamline'.

3 Use the palette knife (or skewer) to 'draw' in circles for the fish eye, gills operculum and streamline down the fish body. When you are satisfied with your fish texture and pasted appearance, tidy the outlines with a damp paintbrush and allow the fish to dry for a few hours. Use the back of the spoon to 'butter' the rest of the board with a thicker layer of mixed plaster, crete stone, glueand shellac flakes right up to the edge of the fish design. It should look as though the fish has been embedded in the surrounding rough textured plaster with bright gold fragments of shellac glinting in it. Press small shells randomly into the plaster before it sets.

4 Wipe away any plaster that has been accidentally worked over the fish body with the paintbrush. Clean the edges of the design and allow to dry thoroughly overnight. Use old toothbrushes to spread the fish and surroundings thickly with different tones of shoe polish. I used neutral on the light areas of the fish and the plaster surround and grey and black polish to emphasize the outlines and details of the fish.

5 Leave the board to dry for about an hour. Buff gently with a soft cloth for a smooth sheen on the fish body and lovely, crusty, rocky look.

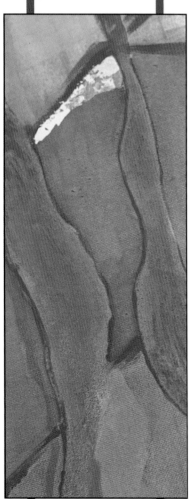

Sunscape

Not awfully sure how this painting was going to end up, I started by pouring glazes of yellow ochre, rust and blue across the canvas, leaving a large area of white showing across the top. When this was dry, I added more texture to the canvas with rollers in the same colours. Whilst most of the rolling was done vertically and horizontally, I also rolled the brown and ochre heavier towards the bottom, suggesting hill shapes. When I really looked at what I had done, it reminded me of a large sun shape I often used when designing tapestries, so I drew it in, in pencil. The shallow "mountain" lines were added and painted with rust paint and reactor. More depth was created by painting darker ochre and orange around the bottom of the sun. The sun itself was painted in yellow, with orange detail. Thin blue mountain shapes, painted above the rust mountains, mimic their shape. Thin brown detail lines were added with a paintbrush, in a painterly way around the shape of the sun. I still felt that the sun shape needed to be highlighted, so I added some variegated gold leaf in small amounts, and then painted shellac over the sun area only. I varnished the rest of the painting, excluding the rust paint, with a water-based varnish. The result is an unusual painting with a number of different textures and effects, from matt to shiny.

Expe(red)iment

Experiments often end up looking rather nice and sometimes even better than the finished work they were meant for. While costs may escalate, it's a good idea not to scrimp too much when doing them – you could end up with a number of amazing works of art you never bargained on. Somehow, the psyche loosens up as it knows that the outcome of one's exploration is incidental – a means to an end.

This painting was just such an endeavour: It was painted on a home-made canvas, stretched onto a stretcher frame which I was given to me years ago, and which has been quite useful. I used various techniques, which I wanted to try out on other paintings. The process was much the same as that in the other red canvas (see page 82), using only one strip of tissue paper. The only additions were the use of an extra ochre glaze in the background and crackle glaze in the vertical ochre area. For something different, the artwork is displayed on the stretcher frame.

(see page 82)

i like
red
it dances
for me ...
Alexandre Arnau

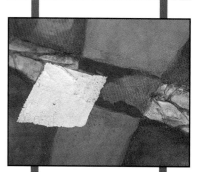

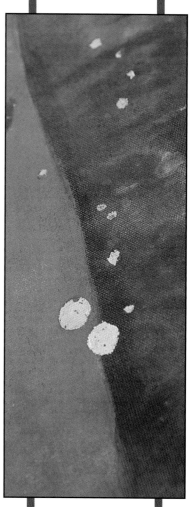

The other side of the sun

A large white canvas can be a bit daunting at the best of times, so a good ploy is to divide it into sections – this can almost automatically create its own picture. All you need is an interesting background, a bit of texture and some detail – read on …

You will need

Ready-made canvas
Paintbrushes
PVA: White, yellow, orange, varying shades of red, magenta and purple
Scumble glaze
Rust paint and activator
1 sheet gold leaf
Tissue paper (I used the thicker, florists' variety)
Cold glue, watered down 1:1
Pencil
Spray bottle with water
Denatured alcohol (methylated spirits)

1 Dilute white PVA with water about 1:1 and paint onto the canvas. Allow to dry.
2 Draw the pattern onto the canvas (see template on page 127). Paint glue into the areas where you want to place the tissue paper. Press strips of tissue paper onto this glued area. Do not try and smooth it out – you want lots of texture.

3 Paint glue on top of the tissue paper and allow to dry. Mix the various shades of yellow, orange and red into glazes, using 2 parts glaze to 1 part water, 1 part paint. The amount will depend on the size of your canvas. I used a tablespoon as a measure. Spray the canvas lightly with water, lay it flat and drip the various colours onto it.
4 Spray with water. Then lift the canvas up and allow the paint to run, turning every few minutes, so that the entire surface is eventually covered. If the glaze is not inclined to run, spray with water again. Too much water will give a faded effect. The glue on the tissue paper will resist the glaze, so you may need to help coat these areas with a paint brush.

5 When it is covered in glaze, lay the canvas flat again, and drop alcohol onto the wet surface. This will form circles, the size of which will depend on the thickness of the glaze and the amount of meths used. The thinner the glaze, the more effective the meths. Allow to dry.
6 Using the magenta and purple glazes, add darker shading with a paintbrush in the following areas: around the edges of the canvas, above each of the tissue paper stripes, and around the large sun area.
7 Add stripes of rust paint underneath the tissue paper stripes and the large sun area. Follow the manufacturer's instructions. Alternatively you could paint in a mottled dark brown and yellow stripe.

8 When dry, glue the appropriate areas, and whilst still tacky, add gold leaf.

9 Varnish, though not over the rust paint, as this will change its look.

Aloes in-flame

I have long been fascinated with what constitutes paint and the origins of pigments. I first fell in love with the rock paintings of the ancient Khoi and San peoples while exploring the mountain caves of the Eastern Cape as a teenager and young adult. It amazed me that so-called primitive people could accomplish such exquisite and weather resistant work. How did they do it? As I gave voice to my wonder so the beginnings of answers slowly began arriving.

Gifts of crumbling old Pharmacopoeia and early settler's household recipe books (with advice from skinning sheep to the many uses of whiting) were passed on through my dad and devoured by me. I copied San art onto stones, rocks, water features and restaurant walls, but the modern paints I used just couldn't capture the same effects. Recently many friends who know of this particular interest have added to my library with more histories of primitive paintings and tomes of formulas for paint making, histories of colour and recipes for home-made paints.... And I'm still learning that individually we don't know very much in spite of our easy access to information.

But to honour these contributors I feel I can now include this project based on my very own kitchen concoctions which work very well!

The natural earth colours of readily available cement oxides from the local building supplier immediately suggested I paint the aloe plants that abound in my garden. Aloe flowers, like bright flames, add warmth to the winter landscape of the Eastern Cape and are now the designated provincial flower. To suit the winter flame theme I made a simple fire-screen by hinging three MDF panels and base-coating them with iron oxide paint as a backdrop for the aloe painting.

You will need

Yellow, ochre, red and green oxides used for cement colouring (I used less than 1 t of each as pigment for the paints and I still have leftovers)
1 egg
Yoghurt
Talcum powder
Fine and medium artist's oil-paint brushes
An aloe design chalked onto base-coated panels suitable for a fire screen (see template on page 125)
Rust paint and oxidising agent (or use sand in glue to create texture instead)

1 Separate the yolk from the white of the egg. Mix teaspoons of yolk with a teaspoon each of yellow, ochre and red oxides. This will make more than enough coloured paint for the flowers in this project. Beat the egg white a little with a fork to loosen it and add enough talcum powder to make a dense white paint. Mix enough green oxide powder with two tablespoons of old yoghurt to form a dense green 'milk' paint, the consistency of thick cream.

2 Paint the aloe flowers and stems with rust paint. Allow to dry and recoat only the flower heads with rust paint for a coarse texture. Paint on oxidising agent and allow rust to develop (alternately use fine and coarse sand in glue to get a similar effect).

3 Paint the aloe leaves in egg white and talc paint. This will dry quickly. Leave the base coat, showing where shadows occur on underlying leaves in the design. This will create natural shading when green is painted over later.

4 Paint the flower stems in yellow and ochre egg paint.

5 Paint the base of each rusted aloe flower in short thin strokes, using yellow egg paint. Work up towards the point of each aloe flower, adding layers of ochre and red egg paint using the same short thin strokes with a fine brush. Taper the flowers to their tips with plain red egg paint. If the flower colours on top of rust are too muted, add a little talcum powder to some of the mix for opacity. Allow the talc-egg-paint to dry and then recoat with the original coloured egg mixes for clarity.

6 Paint in the leaves, using the green milk paint. Work the paint in long lines in the direction of the leaves' growth. To add extra shading down the centres and sides of the leaves, mix a little left over red egg paint into the green milk paint to deepen the colour. Scratch in any thorny edge details on the leaves with a skewer or paint brush handle.

For a final touch you can seal the painting with liquid wax: use beeswax softened with heat and mineral turps or neutral shoe polish.

Hint: These home-made paints look wonderful, but can smell horrible! Do not try to keep them longer than a day or two. They do lose any offensive odour once dry, however. The results are very satisfying – no sulphurous sniff or sour stench – so they are worth the effort and are certainly the most affordable paint you can get!

Here comes the sun (paint)

With its roots in the 160-year old cyanotype or "blue printing" process, sun paint offers a much easier and uncomplicated approach to creating a similar effect. Sun paint (pigment dye) is made up from fabric-paint pigment, but instead of having an emulsion base; it is mixed with a liquid fixer, which binds it to the fabric.

The minute I decided to get stuck in and do this project, we had the rainiest season in a long while – and you do need the sun! Fine, I thought, Angie can do this in PE – they had floods! Eventually we were graced with two lovely days and voila – it worked. The whole apple cart was very nearly upset by Moby Dick (our large white cat), who decided the strelitzias were just right for scratching a cat's head – but that's another story! With sun overhead and all the stuff in hand I dashed outside at midday (that's the best time), to spread out my cotton fabric on a board (the grass will give a slight texture).

Pleasantly between the showers, the sun gushes down.

William Cullen Bryant

I used blue sun paint with some magenta added as the blue on its own is very tyrquoise. I sponged the fabric with water and then brushed on my paint mixture (slightly diluted to make a softer colour). The strelitzias were placed on top of the wet fabric and then left there until the fabric was dry. When removed, the lighter impression of the strelitzias remained – something like tanning with your sun glasses on! I stretched the fabric over two frames and my quick art was ready to hang.

This is a wonderfully easy thing to do, and anything can be used to block the sun. Nature supplies lots of inspiration but you could also use paper cut-outs, stencils – I've even seen something done with a hammer and nails!

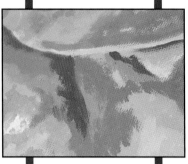

Desert rose

One of my best gifts ever was a digital camera, which works overtime! This project was worked from a photo I took of an echeveria growing in Angie's garden. On first glance, many of the aloes and succulents appear a single colour, but if you really look at them, there are a range of the most beautiful subtle shades. The echeveria, though, is quite colourful, however you look at it! While the painting process wasn't necessarily that quick, due to the size of the canvas, it was an easy way to create a shaded-looking picture, using flat colours. I posterized my image using Photoshop on my computer and used this as a reference to reduce the photo to become more or less a colouring-in exercise *a la* paint by numbers! I cheated more by enlarging the printout on a plan copier and traced it onto the canvas (see template on page 126). Whilst there is no shading, I tried to keep the colours as close to the original as I could. I was also not very careful with the edges of each colour segment, but allowed the colours to blur and blend into each other.

Hitch up your camera, if you're lucky to have one, and take as many photos as you can. Be aware of the world around you, down to its smallest detail, and you'll never be short of inspiration.

A rose by any other name

PVA is not the best medium to use when trying to shade a picture, as it dries so quickly, but I thought I would give it a bash anyway. (Add scumble, if you have, to slow down the drying rate.)

This panel was painted in ordinary PVA using white, stone and red. No mixing of colour was done beforehand – only on the board while painting.

After priming, the flower was drawn onto the Supawood board in pencil (see template on page 125) and the stone background filled in with a paintbrush. To make it more manageable, before the paint dried, the petals were painted one at a time. The darkest areas of each petal were painted in red, quickly adding white, so that a shade of pink was created by blending the two. More white was added as it was needed, making the pink lighter, thus creating the highlighted areas. The centre was painted in stone with the detail added in a mixture of red and stone. Plain red dots were added as a final detail.

> I'll paint what I see – what the flower is to me, but I'll paint it big and they will be surprised into taking the time to look at it.
>
> *Georgia O'Keeffe*

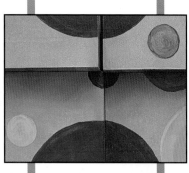

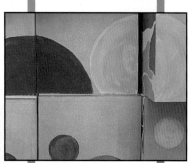

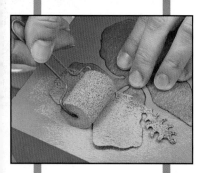

Flower power

After a major cleanup in my youngest son's room I had to find a new home for his building blocks. This gave me the idea for this pop art project which can be changed around at will. There are endless combinations for you to try.

Mostly based on stencilling, the idea for the motif came from a rather lovely hibiscus tree outside my music teacher's room. The tree bears beautiful single white hibiscus flowers, which always catch my attention. I took some photos and used my computer to help do a colour separation for the multiple stencil of the large flower.

A stencil is nothing more than a simple shape cut out of card or plastic and is a quick method of repeating a design. Stencils can be positive (the desired shape is cut away – the 'windows' form the motif to be used), or negative (the stencil forms a block-out, and the area around the stencil is painted). The simplest or single stencil has the complete design on one sheet, and is usually painted in one colour. More complex or multiple stencils may need a separate stencil for each colour, and would be laid onto the surface one after the other so that the image is built up. Multi-colour stencilling looks more three-dimensional than simple stencils.

You will need

Wooden cubes 150 x 150 mm
Small rollers – one for each colour
Paint brushes
Masking tape
PVA paint in white; orange; lime; turquoise; blue; pink
Stencils: Small negative flower stencil; 3 sizes of positive flower stencils; large multi-colour stencil (templates on page 123); negative circle stencils in various sizes
Water-based varnish

Preparation and hints

- Prime the cubes all over with white PVA and leave to dry. Use a roller to apply paint unless otherwise stated.
- Before painting the designs, mask around the top edges of each cube to prevent paint seeping over and onto another side.
- The nine cubes are placed together and each side painted as one panel with the exception of the single hibiscus (side one). Allow each side to dry thoroughly before doing the next.
- When painting the second and subsequent panels it is important that the blocks of the previous panel are all facing the same way.
- As a precaution against scratching I used a soft towel on my work surface, and varnished each completed panel with water-based varnish before continuing.

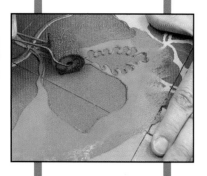

Side one

Paint one side of each cube in a different colour, using a roller. You have nine cubes and five colours, so duplicate some colours or use more colours. Leave to dry. Using a negative stencil with the shape of a flower as a block out, paint a different colour around the stencil. The flower will be the colour you originally painted the side. Repeat on each box and leave to dry.

Side two

Paint one side of all the blocks lime green and leave to dry. Stencil in one large flower using a roller. Stencil in 3 medium flowers in different colours, randomly spaced. Add a host of different coloured flowers, using the smallest stencil. Leave to dry thoroughly before moving on to the next side.

Side three

Place negative circle stencils onto the cubes and paint the background around them in orange. Allow to dry, remove the circles and fill in the blanks with a brush, creating a slight texture. If you do not want to go to the trouble of using stencils, paint the cubes orange, allow to dry and paint coloured circles on top, though the orange will then affect the colours used for the circles.

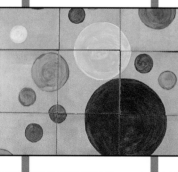

Side four

I have used a block-out and three-part stencil for this. If you do not want to stencil, simply trace the pattern and colour in. The stencil can be approached in two ways:
• Paint the blocks orange and the background turquoise after placing the large negative stencil in place; or
• Place the negative stencil in position first, paint the background turquoise, and fill in the orange with a brush.
Place the second colour stencil in position, and fill in with red. The third colour is magenta. The details are painted in purple (mix blue and magenta).

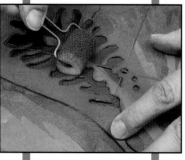

Side five

With orange, roll a stripe along the left side of each set of three cubes, creating three evenly spaced stripes. Repeat this at 90°. Do not press too hard – you want an 'evenly uneven' line and not a solid one. If you do prefer a more solid check, then continue as for side six and repeat the same process crosswise. Repeat this process with the red, magenta, blue and lime, moving in about one roller-width each time.

Side six

Align the cubes once again – the end is in sight! Place varying widths of masking tape across them at random intervals. You can place some of the masking tape alongside the strip next to it. The space between the masking tape will be the width of your stripes. Make sure that you leave open areas more or less evenly across the cubes, so that the colours will eventually be evenly spread. Paint in the area you have left open with one colour. Allow to dry, remove some of the tape and paint in your second colour. Continue removing tape and applying further colours until the entire panel has been filled in. Replace tape where needed, to keep the stripe edges strait.

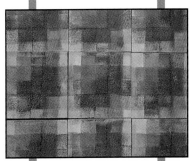

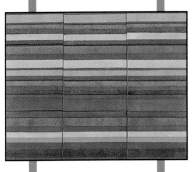

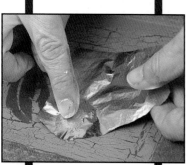

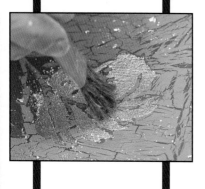

Bare essentials

Not wanting to make this screen too busy with design, I decided to use simple lines: straight on one side and curvy on the other. I have added details with silver leaf and used lots of texture. There are a number of specialized paints around which will give similar textures to the one I have used here, but I decided to make my own with sea sand and PVA. I must have looked like a kid again (I wish!), when I leapt out of the car, bucket in hand, for the sole purpose of collecting the sand.

You will need

Screen with wooden panels cut to size
PVA paint in black, red, dark grey
PVA mixed with scumble glaze 1:1 in stone, dark and medium grey, dark and light teal; red
Crackle glaze
Silver leaf or silver paint
Wood glue
Fine builder's or sea sand
Thick red wax crayon
Paintbrushes
Rollers
Embellishments for the frame
Clear lacquer spray varnish

1 Prime the boards with black PVA. Draw the design onto the boards in pencil. Rework the body lines with thick red wax crayon. Mix fine sea sand into the dark grey PVA and coat the boards with a roller, getting an all-over textured effect. The block areas should be avoided, but don't be too concerned about the wax lines.
2 When the grey texture is dry, scrape away in the area of the wax lines, thus revealing them – I used an old peg. In a patchy way, paint in the red glaze in the background area, (not the figures) using a roller. Leave lots of the grey ground showing. Cover more of the ground in the same way with the medium grey and then dark teal. Repeat this process for the figures, using the stone, medium grey and light teal. Go over the lines into the background area, with the light teal.
3 Scrape away any excess paint that has covered the wax lines. Paint in the rectangles at the bottom of each panel with red PVA – not glaze. When dry, coat with a thick layer of crackle glaze and allow to dry – follow the manufacturer's instructions. Paint over with medium-grey glaze. The direction of the cracks will depend on the direction of the brushstrokes. Do not over-work, as this will damage the effect.
4 When completely dry, stencil the leaf: first in red PVA, allow to dry and then in glue (see template on page 127).

5 When the glue is still tacky, apply the silver leaf carefully. Pat the leaf gently to secure, and brush away any excess. You may find that some of the silver leaf sticks to the crackle glaze in the cracks. Scrape away gently with a knife. If you do not want to use silver leaf, omit the glue and stencil in with silver paint.

6 Finish by varnishing.

Side two was painted slightly differently, though still using rollers. Additional requirements are white glaze, tissue paper, and silver craft-paint.

The boards were again primed with black PVA. The background texture was built up with a roller; using glazes of stone, medium grey, light grey and white. The rolling was done vertically and horizontally only, and not in a haphazard way.

The crackled lines were added, as for the rectangles on the other side: in red first, coated with crackle glaze and finished with grey. I then glued tissue paper in place with watered-down cold glue to add a different type of texture, gluing over the edge of the paper to secure thoroughly. Once the glue was dry, the tissue paper areas were dry-brushed with silver craft-paint, and the relevant areas silver leafed. Finish by varnishing. The screen frame was painted dark grey and embellished with beads.

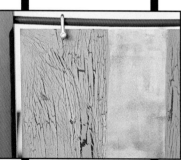

Topsy turf(y)

This homemade canvas was stretched over an old frame I had for another project. It was initially an experiment for colour and also the use of rust paint on canvas. I started by pouring red and ochre glazes across the centre section and allowing them to run. This is a nice way to start a painting.

If you're looking for inspiration, pour paint down the canvas and see what shapes emerge. Add some detail with a bit of shading or embellishments. I applied the rust paint with activator added at different time intervals to see the effect. I then experimented with various crackle glazes – these work more effectively on wood than on canvas.

Gold leaf fragments (skewings) added highlights. The upper section was too light, so I used left-over shellac to varnish the gold leaf and tone down the upper section of the painting. (It was initially the lower section, but I decided the painting looked better upside down – which is now right side up!)

> I've caught this magical landscape and it's the enchantment of it that I'm so keen to render. Of course lots of people will protest that it's quite unreal, but that's just too bad.
>
> *Monet*

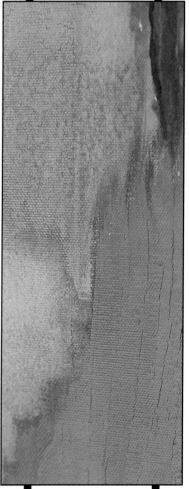

(S)oilscapes

I live with the Grand Helderberg Mountains within view, so the mountainous landscape image was bound to come out somewhere in this book! On my daily meanderings, I am always amazed at how the light changes the mountains at different times, not to mention the weather – sometimes four seasons in one day! I used traditional oil paints in this project, applied with a palette knife. This is also a great way to use up leftover paint from another oil-painting project. You can build up all sorts of interesting effects. If you do not have any left-over oil paint and want to try this project, small tubes are available in sets.

You will need

3 boards (mine are 150 X 300 mm)
Red PVA or acrylic paint
Paintbrush
Range of oil paint colours
Artist's medium to dilute the paints and encourage them to dry faster
Palette knife
Palette
Kitchen towel
Mineral turpentine for cleaning up

1 Prime the boards with red PVA or acrylic and allow to dry. Squeeze a small amount of each oil colour onto your palette. Mix artist's medium into each blob of paint, with your palette knife, in approximately a 1:3 ratio. If you need to, draw a simple picture onto your board (see templates on page 000). There is no space to fiddle, so keep it simple!

2 Start in the sky area in each painting. Pick up a couple of blues and white with your palette knife, and smear them onto the painting, allowing them to mix on the board. Continue like this, adding a little purple, yellow or pink, as the fancy takes you. Fill up the entire sky area, allowing a little red to show through, adding to the effect. If you've been a little heavy with one particular colour, it can be scraped off and something else applied – oil takes a long time to dry, so don't panic.

3 Continue with the mountains, picking up a bit of grey, white and purple on your palette knife and smear onto the board into the appropriate area.

4 The field areas are done in much the same way, using yellows, greens and a little orange and red.

5 Oil takes quite a while to dry, especially if applied this thickly. I recommend waiting a good few weeks before attempting to frame your artwork. Framing is a good idea, as it makes a huge difference to paintings like these.

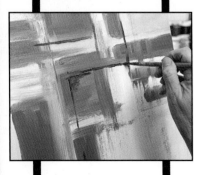

Elementary abstraction

When you next need an original artwork to impress your dinner guests and time is of the essence then this is for you! This painting proves the point that you really don't need much, by way of material or time, to create an original work of art. This canvas took about half an hour and similar works sell for a considerable amount in decor shops! It is based on a variety of browns and white and painted in a very haphazard way.

You will need

Canvas
Student or craft acrylic: white, yellow, red and blue
  (artist's acrylic will also do)
Large brush (size 12)
Small brush(size 4)
Varnish (optional – any kind will do!)

1 Mix a brown with yellow, red and blue. This should have more blue than yellow and red, so that when it is lightened with white, it becomes a mushroom colour. Separate some of this brown and add a little more red to make a red-brown. Picking up white and blue-brown together on the large brush, paint in the outlines of the block shapes.

2 Fill in the background of the canvas by picking up white and brown together and painting it onto the canvas with haphazard strokes. Make sure there is no canvas showing through. The more white you use, the lighter your painting will be, the more blue/brown you use, the more mushroom and the more red/brown, the more pinky!

3 Mix a deep teal colour by adding more blue to some leftover brown and use this, together with the other two browns and white to fill in the block shapes. Don't be precise at all, as this makes the painting stiff. In fact, keep the edges blurred and blur them more with your brush! You want to create interesting streaks by the mixing of the colours on the canvas.

4 Add red highlights with the thin brush and voila! Your artwork is ready to hang. (You can varnish if you like). If you don't like what you've painted, since this is acrylic paint and quite opaque, you can paint everything out and start again. But you need to cook now, so leave that for your next dinner party!

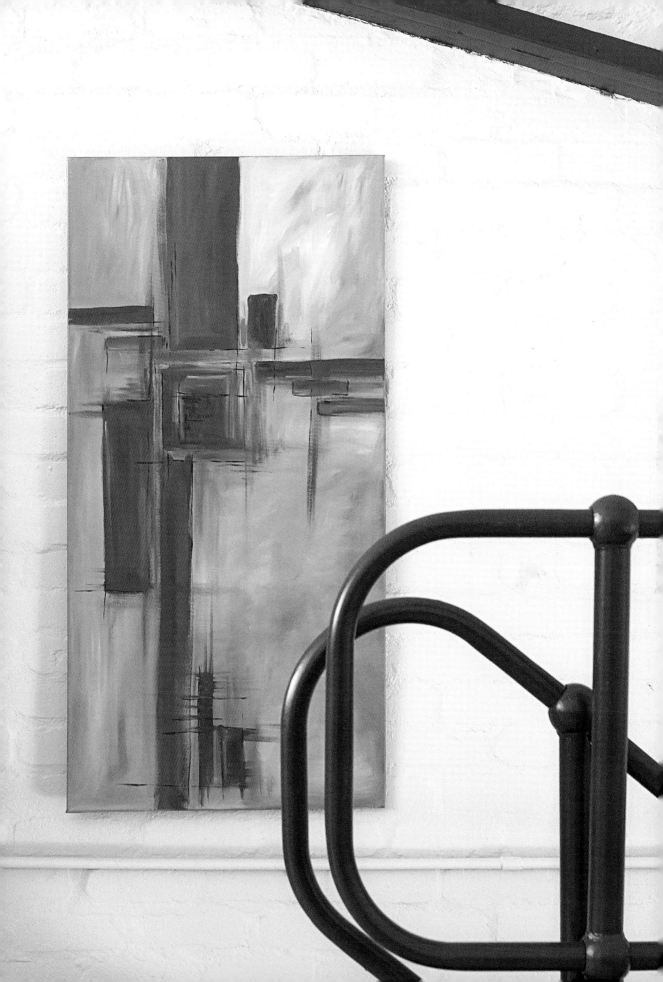

Enc(rust)ed criss-crosses

Between my dad and my friendly carpenter I have many wood off-cuts to put to good use. A simple project is to make up painted and decorated cross pieces. These have become a hot décor item and look great grouped together, whether symmetrical or not. I primed all these plain wooden crosses with rust-paint under-coat. Depending on the manufacturer, this can be black, maroon or brown oxide-based paint. It grips well on plain wood and is a great background colour for over-painting with rust and copper paints.

On two of the wooden crosses I experimented with rust paints – basically different grades of iron filings in paint base. (Use steelwool to create these easily at home.) Rust paints are sold with oxidising agents to activate the rust. Manu-facturers recommend sealing the rust as soon as it has developed to the degree you like. I fancy just leaving it for a truly authentic weathering effect. Household cleaners, degreasers, salts, caustics and corrosives are among the various agents I experimented with to develop rust more quickly than simply exposing metal to air and water. This time I glued and stapled interesting bits of rusty cans to add rusted colour and detail to the crosses.

One cross has a rectangular centre piece, which was a test sampler for shellac, in clear varnish and PVA. It just worked with a squashed beer-can bottom stuck in the middle of it, all topped off with another flat abalone bead. More abalone buttons make a feature of the cross-arms together with stick-on lead caming used in fake stained glass. The other rusty cross has the beer-can top stuck in the middle on top of a tuna-can lid which was edged with stick-on copper tape – the kind used by real stained glass artists to edge sharp pieces of glass before soldering them together. This cross, too, was finished off with the bright copper-coloured abalone buttons and beads.

I used natural blue-green paua shells to decorate a smaller, symmetrical cop-per-painted cross, together with rectangular mirror-mosaics, more stick-on copper tape, silver wire, lead caming and a sample tile from another project.

More copper tape was used to edge another tile sample, which was too pink to include in the red kitchen-project. To focus on the pink I encrusted the ends of each arm with crushed pink glass for glitz and used a glitter glue blob to add a red spot to each end. Beach sand in glue added a light brown which echoed the colour of tiny mosaics cut from 3 mm MDF. There's quite a story attached to these little squares. I've been well trained by my dad (and my carpenter friends) to work in mm rather than the more familiar use of cm from my sewing and quilting background. I had drawn an elaborate cutting plan with all sizes in mm for my local hardware supplier to cut. When I came to collect the 100 mm pieces I thought I had ordered, the dear man had also painstakingly cut these cute little 10 mm squares – he thought I'd probably made a mistake and meant cm but he knew how weird artists can be so decided to play it safe and cut both! So what could I do but use them for something special? They look good placed diagonally together with some pretty polished ag-ates along each arm of the cross.

The final cross in this grouping was given a shiny polished gleam of gold and silver as a foil to all the rusted metal. The cross was primed with red oxide before concentric circles of stencil glue were painted onto it. When this had dried to a tacky finish I applied gold leaf and skewings to the glue and brushed off the excess into my skewings container. I then used gold and silver spray paint in a way not included in the manufacturer's instructions. I sprayed the paint at very close range directly into the spray can lid and used a thin water-colour brush to apply the liquid metal paint from the lid to the cross between the concentric gold-leaf circles radiating outwards. This gave a satisfyingly rich metal-finish to the cross and dried almost instantly.

T(rust)ed tartan

I painted a sample block to experiment with various home-made and manufactured rust paints and oxidising agents. Some claim to produce different colours of rust. I needed to test these before using them in the various projects. I painted parallel bands of rust paints across the board. I then painted the oxidising agents in parallel

stripes from top to bottom at right angles to the bands of rust paints and waited for the rusty checks to develop.

I took careful note of which paints and agents produced which effect so that I could use it as a reference tool. But a friend visiting was so much struck by the criss-cross effect I decided to use it as an archetypal cross design by outlining an asymmetrical cross across it with shiny brown stained abalone buttons, interspersed with rusted metal mosaics cut from a beer can with the pull tab added for good measure. The completed board needed a frame of sorts, so I stuck it onto a larger oxide-coated board and added a few interesting rusty bits brought by my beachcombing friends. (Thanks, Lindsay and Sarie.)

I, too, scrounge interesting rusty beer cans and odd unidentifiable objects from beach debris and other dumping sites. Beer and soft drink cans are wonderful to work with, as the metal is so thin it can easily be cut into shapes with a pair of scissors dedicated for the job. The pieces are easy to beat flat with a hammer as well. This is great for working off frustration and turning negative into positive energy – and one feels so virtuous and cunning to be recycling discarded rubbish into sought-after art works!

Finger food for the soul

Functional art. Earth-toned labyrinth placemats can double up as wall art. Labyrinths have been around for thousands of years as evidenced from ancient spiral-stone engravings found world wide. These archetypal art forms obviously resonate deep within the human psyche. A recent distinction defines a labyrinth as a unicursal (one route) pathway which one follows as opposed to a maze which is multicursal and designed to make you choose routes (and dead ends which frustrate instead of calm!).

The geometry of the spiral is based on an arithmetic progression and is one of the basic structures found in many plants and animal life forms and is the underlying pattern of the traditional labyrinth – and apparently the expanding universe!

I used the simple three-circuit labyrinth design and stretched it to rectangular shape to suit standard-sized place mats. (These mats would be quite effective at calming the souls who have to wait for service at busy fast-food restaurants. Instead of drumming the fingers impatiently, walk the mats and expand your humanity!).

To provide the underlying circular feel to these rectangular labyrinths, I under-painted wood-toned spirals reminiscent of growth rings of cut trees. I chose the earthy colours to over-paint for a warm and inviting effect. These look great protecting a plain wooden surface.

You will need

Labyrinth design

Ready-primed standard placemats: 400 x 300 x 3 mm MDF or Masonite (or recycle those old stained ones you were about to throw out)

Polyurethane varnish or two part epoxy varnish (for extra long life)

Eraser (cheap plastic/rubber type)

Small-sized wall painting brush

PVA in terracotta, teal and maroon PVA (use samples or small amounts of craft paints or artists acrylics)

Acrylic scumble glaze

Felt (optional)

1 Mix glazes from the three colours, scumble and water in the ratio of 1:2:2 parts respectively. Then mix a brown glaze using 2 parts terracotta glaze, 1 part maroon glaze, 1 part teal glaze and 3 parts scumble. Cover a placemat with this brown glaze and, while it is still wet, start in the centre with your brush and sweep a spiral towards (and over) the edge of the mat. The spiral should be subtly coloured like light wood-staining. Do one mat at a time and allow them to dry thoroughly before overpainting.

2 Drag a coloured glaze horizontally across a mat. Wait a minute for the glaze to settle and then use the narrow side of an eraser to trace the rectangular labyrinth

pattern on the wet surface. Try to make the pathways wide enough for two fingers to fit. No problem if you make mistakes – simply re-drag glaze and try again. This is a great exercise in loosening up the right brain (no matter which hand you use) so relax and enjoy drawing and re-drawing with an eraser! Get into a rhythm – this is free therapy!

3 When you are satisfied with your drawn labyrinth, use your finger to trace a pathway through to the centre of the labyrinth. Finger–drawn labyrinths are used for meditation as well as calming and focusing the mind. The action of drawing with fingers from both hands balances the brain and many business people find it helpful to do this before meetings or during intense telephone conferences instead of doodling. It has also been proven as effective therapy for training AD (H) D (Attention Deficit (Hyper-activity) Disorder) sufferers to focus their energy. So WOW! This is a great tool to style as a gift for just about anyone. Wrap one up for your child's teacher as a thank you present!

4 To finish off the mat, drag border lines in a pattern across the short sides. Allow to dry. Varnish with several coats of polyurethane varnish if the mat is to resist heat and scuff marks. Glue felt to the back for perfect presentation and protection.

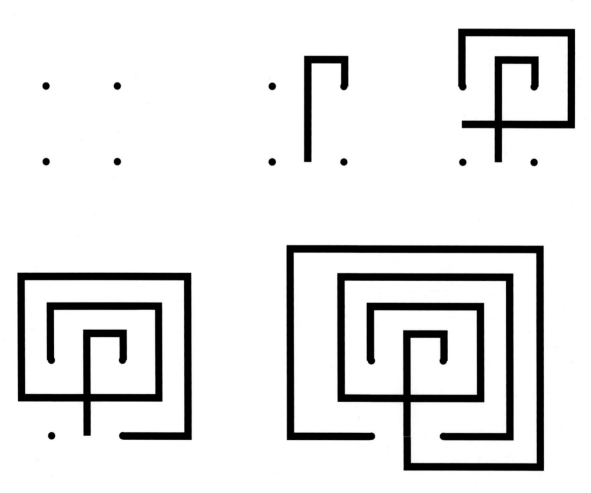

Magnetic personality

The graffiti look is ideal for artwork in a teenager's bedroom and giving a white magnetic board a face lift, is an easy way to create it!

What better materials to use for a graffiti look than spray paint. The magnetic board is very smooth, so I sanded it slightly with fine sand paper to improve paint adherence, and then sprayed on the black outlines of the faces. I used yellow, metallic blue and neon red to add the colour detail. Rather than standing the board up while spraying, I raised it only slightly: the paint would have run due to the smoothness of the board. This created a little bit of a problem with the spray cans, as they are designed to be used upright, but I persevered, clearing the nozzles often. I held the nozzles fairly close to the board so as not to get the paint too far and wide. The black lines became slightly hazy when adding the colour detail, so I redid them when I had finished blocking the colour in. If you want crisper lines, use a series of negative (block-out) stencils.

The funky details added are magnets made from found objects glued onto magnetic strips.

Every child is an artist. The problem is how to remain an artist once he grows up.

Pablo Picasso

Night time

Glow-in-the-dark paint (which I will refer to as GDP) is now available in a range of colours, though the most commonly sold is a pale green which lights up with a ghostly phosphorescence in the dark. It glows strongly directly after exposure to bright light and fades to a faint glimmer after a while. GDP is most effective painted onto a white or light background – in this instance it was painted over white primer. It also glows better and longer if at least three coats are built up. I decided to combine it with black chalkboard paint (which I'll refer to as CBP) for maximum contrast in this city night-scene.

The deceptively simple scene hides a detachable chalkboard-duster as well as a chalk holder. The black board can also be removed, revealing a well known command! The detachable piece will easily be found, if left lying about, by its three guiding stars in the dark! (Paint the reverse of the detachable board also with CBP to record secret messages).

It's a good idea to paint this project at night and keep switching off the light to check the intensity. You'll be amazed at the spots of shiny green gore that suddenly appear on the floor, work surface, your clothes and hands. I felt like one of those forensic scientists who detect bloodstains with a fancy light!

You will need

Two identical sized rectangular MDF boards (one will become the backing board and the other must be cut into three shapes: one x square, one x larger and one x smaller rectangle)

Additional small rectangular MDF off-cuts suitable for city building shapes to fit on the larger cut rectangle

Primer

Brushes and rollers to apply paint

Black chalkboard paint (CBP)

Mineral turps for cleaning

Spray paints in white, gold and silver

Green glow in the dark paint (GDP)

Small peel-off sticky labels

Small rectangular pieces of sponge foam for stamps

Industrial strength glue (the kind used to glue shelves to the wall)

Glow-in-the-dark sticker stars (mine came from a friend in Luxembourg in 1986, were lost and then found again carefully stashed in a book just before this project 20 years later!)

Small battery-operated touch-light

Velcro fastening tape

1 Prime all boards, including off cuts. Paint the backing board and three cut boards with black CBP. The square board needs to be painted on both sides, as it will be-

come the removable chalkboard. Allow the chalkboard paint to dry overnight and re-coat. Let it cure another day before working further.

Hint: CBP needs thorough and frequent stirring while you work as it settles into a gluey lump as soon as it can rest.

2 Meanwhile cut and stick small labels in rows onto rectangular off cuts as window shapes for buildings. These will act as 'block out' stencils. Leave some spaces blank for effect. Spray paint the 'city building blocks' in various mixes of white, gold and silver and allow them to dry. Peel off the stickers and paint or stamp GDP in the 'window' spaces. Build up a few coats of GDP for maximum glow effect.

3 Paint your 'TIDY UP!' message in white undercoat just above the centre line of the backing board. Allow to dry and paint it again in GDP using at least three coats.

4 Wipe the touch-light cover with lacquer thinners. This etches the plastic roughening it for easy paint adhesion. Dab the cover with two patchy coats of GDP. This will glow as a moon with craters on its surface.

5 Assemble the chalkboard by gluing the small and larger rectangular chalkboards in top and bottom position on the backing board. Leave a space to fit the removable chalkboard between them. Use industrial strength glue, as these boards are heavy.

6 Check that the removable board fits comfortably in the space over the 'TIDY UP!' lettering. Glue corresponding Velcro hook and loop strips on the backing and removable boards for easy placement. Allow the glue to set at least 24 hours before joining the strips or putting pressure on glued pieces.

7 Assemble the city by gluing the spray- and GDP-painted buildings in position.

8 Stick the stars and touch-light moon in position, switch off the main light and away you glow!

Suggestion: Make a chalkboard duster by gluing the hook side of Velcro strips to each short end of the back of a suitably-sized painted building-piece. Glue one piece 10 mm in from the edge. Glue a thick layer of felt between the Velcro strips (much thicker than the Velcro but no thicker than 9 mm). To assemble your duster and chalk holder you also need two 6 or 9 mm scraps of MDF the same size as the Velcro strips. Glue the loop side of the Velcro to these scraps. Place the two Velcro-covered scrap-pieces horizontally between two longer-sided buildings so that when the detachable duster is placed in position it will cling by means of the corresponding Velcro strips. The end which has the Velcro stuck 10 mm in from the edge will fit on the 'top' of a building. Behind this will be a little space which forms a pocket for holding pieces of chalk vertically!

Chalkboard city

If you don't want to fuss with painting bits of MDF and glow-in-the-dark paint there is a much simpler and just as funky option: try jazzing up a plain message board for the kitchen by adding ceramic border tiles to imitate a city scene. I found these at a builder supply warehouse and was so struck by their interesting glazes, colours and patterns that I sat on the concrete floor and spread them out to choose some. In the end I bought one of each in the colour range (at no small price!) and took them home to play some more. These are easy to stick onto any surface, using multipurpose industrial strength glue. You don't need tile adhesive or grout to use them for artistic purposes! I put them onto a backing board painted with black chalkboard paint – the colours suit most tiled kitchens.

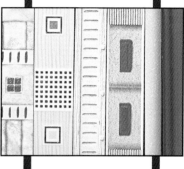

Gate-ways

After opening the book with a door, we thought this gate would make a fitting close. This was a serendipitous find, lying abandoned at the 1st Durbanville Scout hall, I knew immediately I could do something with it. Michael rolled his eyes and groaned at yet another piece of junk being added to the garage hoard! But he's now most impressed at its transformation and was more than happy to hang it in an awkward but appropriate spot.

You will need

Gate with bars as frame – or link panels with twisted wire *a la* barbed fencing
3 mm MDF cut into strips
PVA in white, black
Paint brushes
Metal ruler
White chalk
Compass or other sharp instrument
Cutting tools (rotary cutter and mat work best)
Wire and wire cutters
Drill
Pliers
Very rough sandpaper (grade 40)
Aluminium foil
Corrugated cardboard (painted black)
Mosaics and other interesting found objects in metallic colours
Strong multipurpose adhesive
Copper fabric-paint liner
Clear lacquer-spray

1 Arrange panels in a block and prime with white PVA using rough brushstrokes. These will show through later. Allow to dry and paint black with rough brush-strokes.

2 Draw borders and details of your design using a ruler and white chalk. Fill in design areas with white paint. Add a second coat when dry and allow to dry thoroughly. Sand each panel roughly, creating a distressed look.

3 Mark vertical lines and scratch in using a metal ruler as a guide. Roughen these lines with a sketchy freehand for effect. Add copper lines where desired to highlight the design.

4 Cut triangles in aluminium foil and black corrugated cardboard. Glue in place. Spray with clear lacquer and allow panels to dry. Glue mosaics and found objects where desired.

6 Drill holes where required and assemble using short lengths of wire twisted to the front as for barbed fencing (use pliers).

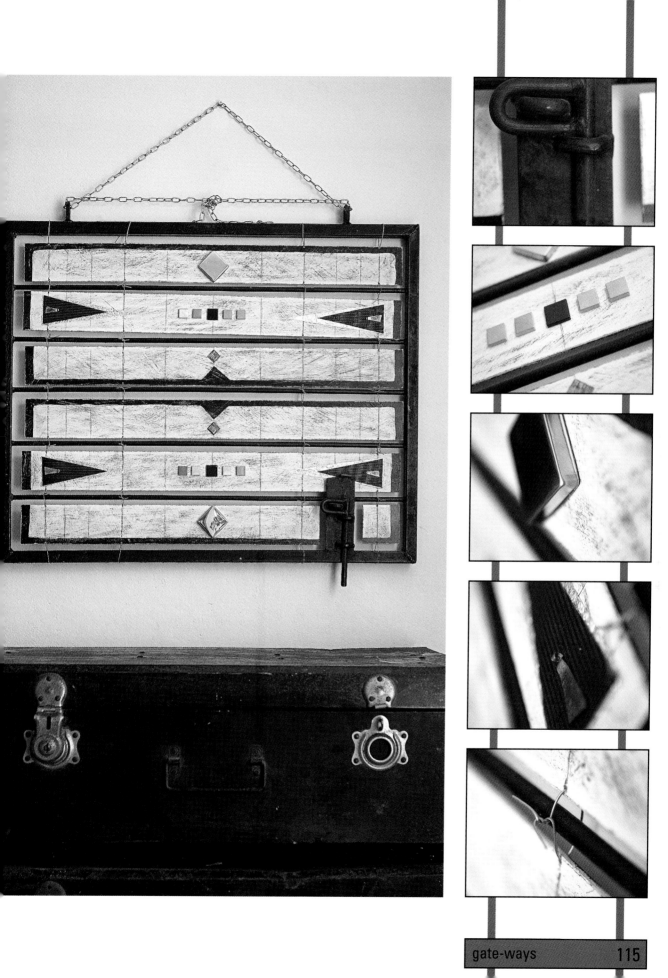

Art happens!

As a final fun project we decided on some live action to jazz up the life of our long-suffering photographer, and test the patience of our understanding publisher! Try making your own art happening – all you need is a large canvas and an even larger ground-sheet and left-over paint. We used some wonderfully simple techniques which we called:

1 "Spilt and Tilt" (pour close up and then tilt the support for the paint to run),
2 "Flat and Splat" (paint poured or thrown from a height onto a flat support) and
3 "Swirl and Twirl" (adding spiral detail with paint from liner-bottles) will finish off your happening with a grand gesture!

In response to the question "How do you know when you're finished?" Pollock replied "How do you know when you're finished making love?" Remember to sign your work with a flourish – who knows, you may be the next Jackson Pollock.

The last word

So ... what is art?

In our quest to answer this age-old question we instinctively turned to various dictionaries where definitions were as dry as "an activity through which to express particular ideas" or that it "implies a personal, un-analysable creative power". There is no arguing with either of these quotes but there is certainly more to it. It is not an exact science, but invention.

Art should stop you in your tracks for a second look and draw you in for a third or more, but perhaps, art is simply seeing the extraordinary in the ordinary and making it dance before your eyes. We think it is – but does it really matter? As long as you like it!

We don't know if we've answered much of this question, but we've sure had a lot of fun and experience trying – we hope this book has inspired you too. If in your trying, you feel you make 'mistakes', take heart and learn. Art is not about perfection – it's mostly about the journey.

Templates

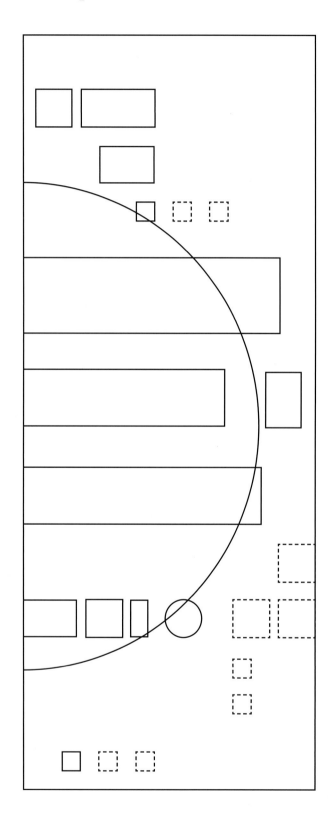

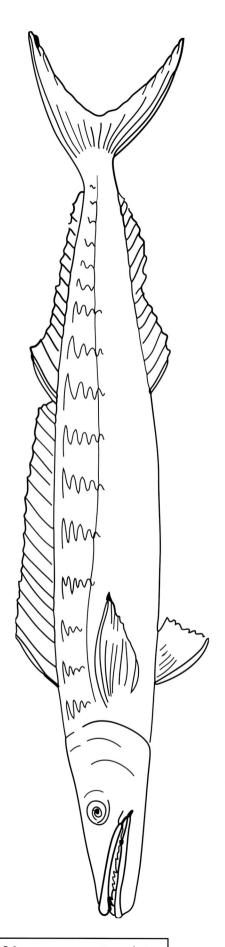

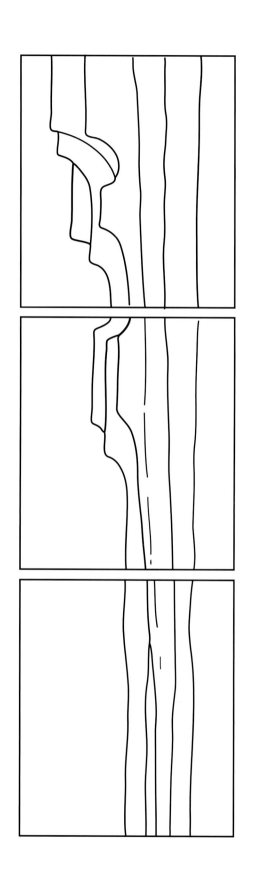

templates

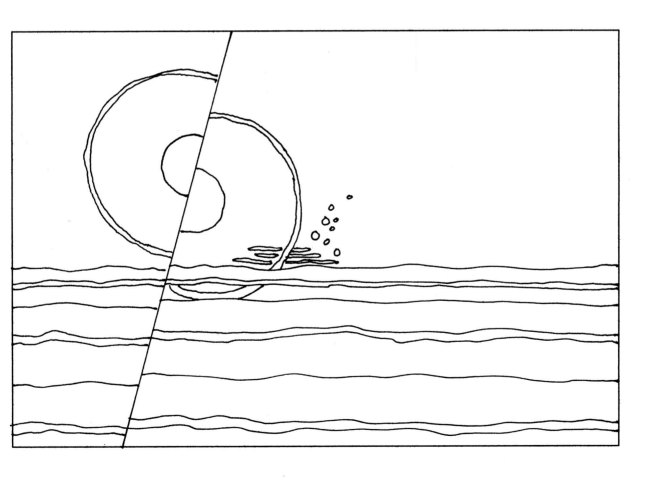

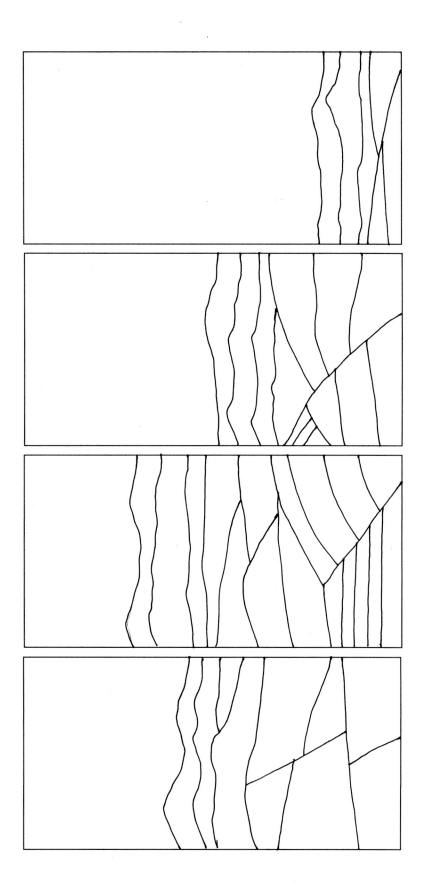